RAMPANT DOUCHEBAGGERY

THE DEATH OF THE AMERICAN GENT

ESSAYS

JAMES COGAN

CONTENT

PROLOGUE

I'm in the holding cell while they run a search for my past crimes. My girlfriend of two disastrously long months is back home, ready to record our convo upon my return.

How did I get here, for the love of god? What circuitous route led to this particular deliverance?

And I'm supposedly 'one of the good ones'. My journey, while Homeric, has for certain not been heroic. But maybe asking for help in the context of American men of a certain age and bent is legit brave. My ego tells me that's exactly right.

Reader, what you're about to uncover is one man's take on the shifting tectonic plates of contemporary culture, beliefs, and behaviors of a broad swath of white heterosexual American men. Online dating, porn, technology, female emergence–all of it percolates in the deep fryer of our national psyche.

Behold tales of muddled manhood in the USA. Fellas, take a look in the mirror and get back to me.

James Cogan
Chicago 2024

CHAPTER 1
RAMPANT DOUCHEBAGGERY

WHEN DID AMERICAN MEN STOP TRYING?

The American gentleman has up and died—skidded right from the Rotary Club to the strip club in three generations.

As the centuries aged from twenty to twenty-one, "dad jokes" became a desultory trend, while young men devolved into spectators rather than participants in life around them—viewers, not doers. American women, on the other hand, sprouted wings. Culturally and politically ascendant, ever more vocal about goals, desires, and injustices, they rapidly rose into the largest group of business entrepreneurs on the planet.

With the massive growth of internet and computer technology, men grew more insular, more divided, less social. But something else happened. American men lost their compass, their old schoolness, their *decency*. Toward the end of the last century— you know, the American Century—the term *douche* creeped into the lexicon to mean a type of male, grew to encompass a demographic, then became the zeitgeist. This book is a Hail Mary attempt to shore up a decency deficit in single, nearly middle-aged men.

Increasingly, it seems, single or divorced American men are porned out, teched up, and dumbed down. With each passing decade, we're more self-involved and less self-aware. Less inclined to be a "good egg." More inclined to snark, empty cynicism, and constant viewing without seeing. Once there was "the sort of man who reads Playboy." Today it's "the sort of douche who sends pics of his junk."

We're sinking in a morass of bros, bruhs, dudes, douches, gamers, slackers, PUAs, MRAs, Chads, incels, alphas, betas, fanboys, tools, and trolls.

Men used to be hesitant to ask a woman her age. Now men ask that same woman if her tits are real.

American women must now confront these uber-troubling realities: Revenge porn. Roofies. Trolling instead of courting.

Pictures of a penis sent to a woman unmet. Do we really need to look any further into our XY gender to see we're dying a Roman death?

Yikes, that's a bit harsh. Yet many men have been leaving the toilet seat of life up, habitually thinking mostly of themselves and maybe someone's bottom line before all else. Wait—isn't this the twenty-first century? Shouldn't American men—formerly world-beaters who defeated villains and built metropolises—be somehow better?

Isn't it time for a new type of American male? One who looks outside of himself? One who, you know, reads and thinks and volunteers and builds stuff that lasts? Why be stuck in a cave, for God's sake?

If you take even a cursory glance at today's media landscape, men behaving badly is at least a small fraction of each day's news cycle, whether it's Wall Street shenanigans or frat house "bros before hos" casual atrocities. Whether it's spewing from online gamers or Silicon Valley tech bullies. This book is not an attempt to "place a microscope on societal ills" or anything that precious. It's merely an attempt to get men of a certain age (thirty to sixtyish) of a certain marital state (single/divorced) to wake the hell up.

The front cover of this book features a man taking the now-cliché photo of himself standing shirtless in his bathroom. It's what's become known on internet dating sites as the "bathroom selfie." It's an epidemic in modern single America—a guy who is wholly unaware of how he appears to the opposite sex. In many instances, the choice is either completely unaware of modern women or hostile to them. Think I'm exaggerating? Ask any—and I mean any—single woman who has spent even a short time dating online. By the way, just so we're clear, "dating online" is an oxymoron.

A woman once related this story. She was on a dinner date with a guy. The woman, a lovely person in her early forties, revered her deceased father, a former attorney. Over dinner, the dude asked her what her late father had done for work.

"He was a lawyer," she said.

"Oh, he was a liar," he said.

Thinking she had misheard, she repeated, "No, he was a lawyer."

Said the dude/douche: "Ah, he was a liar."

True story.

If you're as I was ten years ago, you may, in fact, be thinking, "Here goes another wussy attempt to make men more like chicks"—er, no. Men should be more like gentlemen and less like childish douchebags. Especially in intimate relationships with women, of whom they're often frightened, believe it or not. Why are men so threatened by a species that tussle with directions?

What happened in the past ten-plus years to bolster the belief that a book such as this is necessary? The internet happened, and for men—single men, lonely men—the internet has been very, very bad. I refer you to chapter 4.

So, why me? What are my bona fides, you ask?

Allow me to do a little humblebragging: no one in the history of the internet has spent more time online dating than your scribe. Not one pathetic soul. This primer is the result of ten-plus years of research, literally hundreds of hours of conversations with the

Amys, Lisas, and Kats of the world (steer clear of "Kat"—after date three, you realize with a sigh that she's really still Kathy).

A picture emerges that's recurring and boring. What I've found is perhaps not scientific, but it's nonetheless real. Common traits are heard with dizzying frequency: drunkenness/substance abuse; porn, porn, and more porn; controlling and uncommunicative behavior; major loutiness; anger issues; lack of curiosity about the greater world around them; and deceit. That last one sticks in my damn craw. Even while I'm guilty of it.

"Courting" is as dead as the landline telephone, over which men and women used to converse for hours not so freaking long ago. Wooing the girl, dressing up, being on time, actually making plans, finding out what interests her—all have gone the way of the dodo.

Yet this is not a self-help book. It's more of a how-to book: How to be a grown-up gentleman. How to live a healthier, more aware life. How to sculpt happiness, presuming you define happiness as living joyfully in a healthy relationship with a partner who's the best person in the world for you. Let me repeat: it's the twenty-first century. We need to be better men. To step up. We need to read and travel and volunteer and move beyond our world of whiteness and maleness.

We desperately need to be more curious about the world around us.

It needs to be said before going any further: I've made every single misstep listed in this book, along with a few that are not yet legal in some of our northern plain states. It makes me sad that so many women—who want only that one guy—are repeatedly encountering men who lie and who are casually abusive. Guys who are resentful of modern, successful, single women.

(And lest you think I haven't plumbed the depths of bad decisions, stay tuned. Stay with me all the way to chapter 21, the penultimate chapter and a cosmic rug pull.)

Finally, it's very telling and sorta sad that words such as honor, grace, valor, duty, chivalry, courting, humility, and courage are now viewed through the snark lens.

Ah, the snark lens; the lens of losers. God forbid anyone be earnest.

CHAPTER 2
ONLINE DATING
WELCOME TO THE JUNGLE

Online dating is The Hunger Games with emojis.

It's why the Victorian term *clusterfuck* was invented.

It's the exact opposite of romantic.

It turns smart people into imbeciles.

Like much of the internet, online dating has become a "be careful what you wish for" proposition. It feels like work for most women. Fending off douches is the unfortunate norm. Yet the "ghosting" (when someone you've been in contact with suddenly goes missing), along with the sheer amount of time spent searching/shopping is mind-boggling for most of us.

Nowhere in this brave new world is the distinction between man and woman cast in such stark relief as it is in online dating. The binary difference between men and women's online dating experience is at the core of this book. Most single people over thirty now meet almost exclusively this way. This was the forum that convinced me, a long time ago, that heterosexual American men were not the gentlemen of yore. Online dating is perhaps the primary example of men behaving in ways unrecognizable to earlier generations. Digital dating has rendered the old-school analog dating process inexplicably archaic. That quaint era of mating involved talking, courting, like that.

A woman jumped into the internet pool of allegedly single daters and said this:

"I just got on here a few days ago, but it sure seems to be 'easy come, easy go.'"

Easy come, easy go. You go, girl. You got that right.

The ease of the coming and the going is only a small part of what makes online dating so special, like a brand new level of hell, replete with photos featuring dead animals (men); duck lips (women); phrases like, "Dance like no one is looking" and, "The glass is half full," played on an endless loop, resulting in a psycho-spiritual numbness. Cut with just a titch of low-grade crack.

When most women find the courage to fill out a profile or get tired of being hounded by their besties or daughters to get off the couch and get on a dating site, they initially will politely reply, "Thanks, but no thanks" to the first several hundred messages of, essentially, "Wassup, you look hawt!!"

They'll get this response more often than not from the "spurned" would-be suitor: "You are such a stuck-up bitch!! What makes you think you are so . . ." This is a core example of how men online frequently make life a hellish experience for women. An introductory note sent to my friend Jess: "I'd love to see you hog-tied." Add in the trollers and the young boys posing as older boys, toss in the married men posing as single, stir in the dead fish, guns, and naked torsos, plus the near-constant requests for more, more, more, and you get a kaleidoscopic picture of a fractured, dysfunctional, and seething American manhood.

And if a screenshot is worth a thousand words:

7:37 PM	Are you at the concert?
8:01 PM	Hey
8:07 PM	Please come over and crawl in bed with me after the concert
8:14 PM	The door is unlocked
8:31 PM	If you still love me you'll come
8:32 PM	Just kidding but I want you to get naked and cuddle with me...ok?
8:38 PM	I'm completely shaved right now
8:57 PM	I only have a few requests. you're shaved, you love oral, you get really wet and cam even squirt, and you love me
11:28 PM	Wow...that's quite a message. I am looking for a relationship. Not a booty call. Do not think you and I are on the same page. Take care.

This was sent to a nice, polite, professional woman. After one date and two drinks. OK?

After a certain age, online dating has the breezy desperate vibe of the only game in town. It's efficient and ruthless. Over time you see the same faces, the same tired intros to profiles, and the whole drama about who needs drama least. It's a town where an eight-month relationship is lauded for its longevity. It's where a woman with pictures of cleavage—in every pic—can declare without irony, "If you're gonna make comments about my boobs, you'll be deleted." Self-deception and self-promotion compete for prominence.

Online dating sets you up to fail. Upon first meeting, most women are preemptively musing, "What type of joker will he be?" While the men are arriving either massively over- or underthinking the whole wine-sodden shebang. After a mere six months, online dating turns you into a Buddhist—walking into the next wine bar, you have fewer expectations than Buddha himself. After a series of one-and-done dates, you become conditioned to failure, romantically speaking.

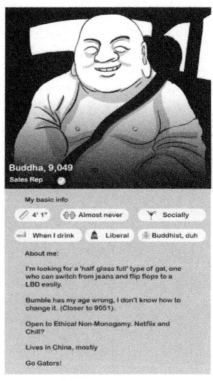

Buddha on Bumble: "Why the fuck are you ghosting me?? Jesus!"

Throw into the mix this fact: one in three women sleep with men they met online on the first date. Add in the one element that makes the internet so maddening: the casual anonymity of the peeps at this corner bar. No one "knows" you—at all. Swill the somewhat less-than-difficult sexual congress in with virtual invisibility, and you've got some bad brew indeed. For men, this is truly putting-out-fire-with-gasoline stuff.

If admin at these dating sites put up a tote board of everyone's deceptions, it'd be a ghost town. But then they'd be out of business. The dating sites are not in the business of busting or policing lies, so that leaves it up to you.

And then there's porn.

The pornification of America is real. Really real. In my research, I've found this: women over fifty rarely watch porn. Women under forty, however, are not porn averse. And men, well, men of all ages and shapes and sizes watch hours and hours of porn. Daily. (See chapter 6, if you dare.) Porn is unhelpful to dating, especially if you're a man in your twenties, thirties, forties, fifties, sixties, seventies, or eighties.

"The easier it is to get sex, the harder it is to find love."

WOMAN ON PLENTY OF FISH
DATING SITE

CHAPTER 3
BADASS WOMEN

American women have not so quietly amped up a revolution that originated in the 1970s. If you haven't noticed, you're not paying attention.

In the past decade, I ran my one and only brick and mortar business, a Yoga studio in Chicago, for eight years. I went from a staff of three to a force of seventeen instructors, mostly women, aged approximately twenty-five to fifty-five. For the first time in my life, I saw a new breed of American woman: the Badass. Just as, for me "cool" isn't what most people think it is–can't be truly cool if you ain't kinda humble deep down–Badass Women are defined by certain characteristics: they're highly functional without fuss or brag, they're not narcissists, and they raise the game on motherhood, mentoring and career by living authentically and intentionally. They consciously pay it forward. So many women I've met in the past decade are kicking ass by being a Badass dame.

Entrepreneurially, culturally, spiritually—and more than ever, politically—contemporary American women are a vibrant force. Consider the collective global influence on women by these one-namers: Michelle, Angelina, Beyoncé, Taylor, Hillary, Oprah, Kamala. Or consider Cher, Gaga, and Madonna. To mistake these ballsy women as mere entertainers is missing the point. Bey, Tay, Cher, Gaga, and Madonna have inspired and empowered women around the planet more pervasively than men know. There are more, and not all are in entertainment—think about soccer and basketball icons Megan Rapinoe and Caitlin Clark, or Serena. Could we have said this in the 1980s? The nineties?

Women in the US today are more diligent, more focused, more career and financially oriented, more curious, more volunteering, more communicative, more collaborative, and, wait for it, more ethical than their male counterparts. That last one was a hard pill to swallow, but stick with me as I make my case.

American women are attempting—successfully—to improve their lives, from abandoning toxic relationships to securing their financial future. Fully invested in the twenty-first century, while the American male still has one foot mired in the twentieth century, the century that his gramps helped shape, once upon a long ago. If you squint, you'll notice that many American men, especially those over forty-five, seem a bit waylaid, hamstrung, rudderless. I say this with compassion but also with urgency: the world needs the American man to be an exemplar of decency, innovation, and courage, whether the world will admit it or not. Consider the global reception given to these men: Kennedy, Clinton, Ali, Reagan, Obama, Jobs, Jordan, Clooney. No other country's visiting dignitaries get the response great American men get. And no one needs the American man to regain his stride like the American woman. Awww. Yet it's true.

American women of all stripes and from all regions—especially college graduates—are living lives that their own mothers, from thirty to forty years ago, could barely imagine. Seemingly over- night women are sponsoring girls-gone-wild spa weekends; hosting bachelorette parties, wine tastings, and book clubs, while piling up stamps in their passports—experiencing so much more fun and true camaraderie than just about anything men are doing today. Yet women are also volunteering, adopting, hiring, traveling, firing, flirting, and stretching themselves, as in run- ning for office. (Clearly we're in the midst of a revolution in the form of women running for political office in the US.) American women are the fastest-growing group of entrepreneurs globally, and more females than men are entering college and the work- force. It's commonly held that the new "knowledge economy," featuring robust careers in design and communications, seem- ingly favors a woman's skill set. Naturally, this threatens men.

But American women didn't rob American men of their power and influence. The men ceded it to them.

Most strikingly, women aren't letting anger dominate their lives. Women ask for help. Females may be more survival oriented than men (it's been said *ad nauseam*) but women today are not merely surviving; socially, culturally, economically, and politically speaking, they're flat out thriving. Look at the restaurants, spas, or bistros of almost any North American city: you'll see women at tables of two, three, four, six. It wasn't that way even as recently as twenty years ago. It raises the question: Where are their male counterparts? What's that? A cave?

One way that women are not thriving? Romantically. One might add "domestically."

TITLE IX

How did this seemingly sudden shift happen? A good place to start would be the 1970s and the Title IX grants that took some funds earmarked for men's athletics and funneled them to funding for women's athletics. This was huge. Suddenly women were not competing against each other, but rather playing on the same team, working toward a common goal—WNBA, anyone? Multiply this by hundreds of thousands of women, at most colleges across the land. Women—for the first time in many cases—were bonding in ways that had nothing to do with looks or men or any of that sexual mess.

What happened to these women? They graduated. They took their majors and their résumés and moved from the campus to the cities and suburbs and got jobs, real jobs with real paychecks and real pressures and real perks.

They got married. They had kids. They ascended in their jobs, multitasking their lives in ways few men have ever encountered. Whether single, divorced, or married, they still assumed major responsibility for childcare and yet found a way to navigate the office—while volunteering. The kids grew up, and the jobs kept increasing in pay and perks and pressure. Sometimes—well, OK, half the time—they got divorced. They bought a condo, a town house. Entered the gym to stay. Learned how to manage their finances. They saw a therapist and worked on what needed adjusting. They took trips to Italy, learned to scuba dive and salsa dance. They joined those book clubs. They learned the difference between Merlot and Pinot Noir, oftentimes during the book club. They moved on and on.

What happened to the men who used to date and marry these women? They didn't "move on." Often they worked harder and harder, earning more money in some cases but not more satisfaction. For the most part, they saw no therapists—because the ex was the problem, right? So they kept repeating the same mistakes, only the drinking and the anger and the bad habits kept piling up. No book clubs for them. No yoga or wine classes. (Besides, a younger chick won't be so damn demanding, amirite?) Pass the Viagra and the smelling salts.

In short, no growth—zero. Right now there are dudes reading the dreaded word growth and deciding to chuck this pansy-ass book across the room.

All the while, culturally, economically, and spiritually, the seismic shift between the genders aged thirty to sixty keeps expanding, surely and swiftly.

CHAPTER 4
I CONFESS, PT. 1: #METOO

Can we talk about me a little?

I've been writing this handy primer in my head for a while. The basic premise—American gentlemen are nearly extinct and are overrun by zombie douchebags—is more pronounced today than when I first entertained this topic so long ago.

You, dear reader, should know one thing right from the jump: I'm no saint. Not a prude, nor a tsk-tsker. Not by a long shot.

I'm a dude. Not merely with a clue but armed with a reservoir of love and support to this day from the man and woman who raised me—my parents. My father, a union carpenter, and my mother, a stay-at-home mom turned realtor, offered me constant love and "good modeling," as they say. It's the greatest good fortune anyone can ask for.

Yet everything in this book, every misdeed, faux pas, snafu, lapsed judgment—the lot of it—I've done. Quite a bit. (You are kindly referred, once again, to the penultimate chapter of this book.)

Been too drunk on a date? Yep. Too angry and judgmental? Check. Let my ego fuel me into really bad decisions? Check and mate.

Am I still making these mistakes? Sometimes, for sure. Not nearly as often as I once did, but yes, and I have to forgive myself when I mess up, which is part of this story.

Two reasons I'm writing this book instead of reading it:

- My beautiful, flawed, goofy, and loving parents.
- I asked for help.

I was living a life of ego, as opposed to essence. My choice in mates was disastrous. The only attributes on my radar for a life-mate could be summed up in the following question: Is she smart, fun, and hot?

Middle west, early '70s

I had no idea who the hell I was.

Fresh out of a failed, brief (but, alas, not brief enough) marriage, I lived with another woman who was wrong wrong wrong. Gorgeous, talented, smart, sexy, and funny, but with serious demons. I loved her desperately, but she ultimately was so abusive—ever had to go to work wearing makeup to cover a black eye?—that I had to arrest her. Like, four times. There is no exaggeration in saying she was on track to stabbing me had I not been advised to evict and arrest her. Like, four times. Horrible trauma, memories that are seared into my very soul.

Yep, #MeToo.

I was at the beach one day during this turbulent period and saw a tall Australian man. I had rented a Hobie Cat sailboat, and he was waiting for my rented boat to return so he could sail. We chatted. I asked him what he did for work as small talk. He told me he was a therapist. I asked him for his number, just in case.

Two months later I went in for a session, which begat two years of intense soul work. At first I rebelled and fought him. Sometimes, in the early days of counseling, I had barely slept the night before, up all night with drink and drugs.

Then I gave in. With his guidance I began to wake up. In short, my life is divided between pre and post therapy. In photos taken pretherapy, I rarely looked happy or even relaxed in any photo, simply because I was not comfortable in my own skin. That's not the same anymore. Therapy was the single best thing I've ever done for myself. I found out who I really am and discovered that I liked the guy I was slowly uncovering.

So began the process of growing into the best version of myself, a process that will never end. I left my cushy gig as college faculty, left my hometown, and moved to a small village where I could see clouds of stars at night. I learned to garden, learned to appreciate the myriad joys of nature. Bought a used sailboat and learned to sail, often hilariously *Gilliganesque*. Began to eat better and get my body moving. Started the life-altering journey of yoga. Got rid of "frenemies" who were decidedly not rooting for me. Simplified my whole damn life. I told myself I was proud of myself. I forgave myself.

I had some "garbage trees" cut down on my property, hardwoods like chokecherry, buckthorn, and box elder, and then I took out all seventy or so tree stumps with my own ax. Took me two years, but each stump untethered from the earth was another step away from the anger and trauma of my recent past.

And then I entered the mind-blowing world of online dating—at the time quite stigmatizing for those of us who ventured into what was a brave new world of cyberromance.

CHAPTER 5

WHAT WANT

WOMEN

This much I know:

Women want a guy who "shows up." What's that mean? If you have to ask . . . OK, women want a guy who'll do what he says he'll do. Steadfast and dependable. You're there, solid.

They want a guy who owns his stuff. As in, "Yes, I'm an independent, but let me explain (with clarity and passion) why."

A guy who is great at his profession—no matter the gig. This is actually a huge misconception that most men have, that women want only a guy who makes tons of money. That's simply not true, and fear is the culprit, as usual. Most women don't give AF what you do for a living, but there are two caveats: be passionate about it, and be damn good at it. Nobody wants a scrub, but show up: dressed well, groomed well, mannered well, with a date planned well.

Women want a guy to be "the guy" without being controlling. I'll let you figure this one out for yourself.

Passionate, yes; obsessive, no.

A guy who isn't afraid to cry. But not crying more than her.

Women adore a man with old-school manners. Not faked courtesy but real chivalry. Refer to chapter 15.

Women want a bit of a bad boy, one who'll occasionally break minor rules that they themselves would not dare; not a lot, just an occasional hint of mischief.

Women love men who are "paying it forward" without anyone knowing.

Men who remember the little things, like your middle name after the second date.

Men who'll lovingly tease them, but only after making her feel truly safe.

See the last part of the last sentence:

Safe. Supported. Really supported . . . and listened to.

A guy who is not cheap. Huge turnoff.

A guy who believes his friends are the best people on the planet.

A guy who is super sweet to his mom.

A guy who never trash-talks his ex(es).

A guy with a twinkle of bad-boy mischief in his eyes.

A guy who volunteers, just because.

A guy who can fix or build things.

A guy who is hygienic without being too "metro."

A guy with a generous heart.

A guy who knows how to have fun—yet knows how to back off—from whatever his passions are.

A guy who views porn not more than they do.

A guy with a passport that has stamps inside.

Shh, still with me? What women really want? Like, really?

Women want a man they can admire. That's it. Admire.

Q: Are you admirable, dude?

Respect. Trust—are you someone that someone can look up to?

No matter the era, no matter the geography, most women still want their guy to be their hero. And heroic isn't necessarily being a soldier or firefighter, or anything that dramatic. Their hero answers a friend's request for help at 3:00 a.m. He does the small things that a man should always do, like run toward those in need, not away.

CHAPTER 6
PORN, PORN, PORN
GET OUT YOUR HANDKERCHIEF

Let's talk about porn. Porn is the silent game changer in American culture. Some have written about "the pornification of America," and it's quite true—*a whole lot of pornifying is going down.*

THE PORN DIVIDE

Porn is very much a generational thing. If you're a female over fifty-five, odds are you watch very little, if at all. If you're a female under forty-five, that's a different story. If you're under thirty, yet another story. See where this is going? If you're a man, then there are two categories: not at all or too damn much.

Porn is the ultimate slippery slope (which may in fact be the name of a porn site). It's hard to wrap the mind around how subtly yet drastically porn is changing our daily life, especially for those younger than forty.

If this chapter is to have any resonance, it's time for me to get real with you, dear reader.

I know porn. I do. Women and men have wholly disparate attitudes about porn (speaking mostly for those over forty). Over-fifty women tend to have the view that all porn stars are scarred, damaged misfits who have serious daddy issues. That many porn stars are "acting." Not so sure about that. What some women miss is the fact that young porn stars love attention, sex, and money. Like, a lot. They've grown up with porn and don't see it as wrong, harmful, or shameful as women over fifty might think. Desiring to be a porn star for many young women is no less stigmatizing than it is for the young man who wants to be a hip-hop star. Porn is nearly mainstream entertainment, another type of video game or online activity to engage in—daily.

Yikes. That's where the problem lies: frequency.

Taking "morality" off the table for a second, porn is damn thrilling. Mind blowing. Wild and exciting. So is jumping from a helicopter onto a mountaintop with only a snowboard on your feet. So is cocaine. These are not activities that you would realistically engage in each and every day. Yet many men, and some younger women, do.

What makes porn so thrilling? It's subjective, of course, but part of it is being privy to goings-on that typically have been private. Some of it is viewing a world that you may wish to experience once in your life but know you never will. Part of it is seeing gorgeous humans behaving like depraved animals. Naughty and nasty, for sure, yet very real in terms of pushing adrenaline.

But here's the thing: it's not a whole lot different from snorting coke. It's very similar in terms of early-stage excitement that over time evolves (or devolves) into something all consuming. All. Consuming. Before you realize it, you're looking at people around you (opposite sex specifically) in a manner you never did before.

You are suddenly seeing people as sex objects instead of as wives, moms, daughters, or coworkers. You're seeing through their clothes. A woman (in a man's case) is completely taken out of her normal—and real—circumstance and thrust onto an imaginary stage with a pole.

Speaking of poles, if you think porn is not radically changing society, how about pole dancing classes? Where do you suppose the current global fixation on butts comes from? How about "twerking"? How 'bout *manscaping*? Notice how younger women currently pose for pics with their tongues hanging out of their mouths? Notice how often they are . . . grinding on each other? That's porn. Tinder is a case in point. Without porn, there is no Tinder, or more accurately, no Tinder culture.

Do you really suppose that the disgusting and pervasive rape culture, found on campus and in the military, is not related to the myriad "gangbang" porn sites that glorify this? In fact, porn in the twenty-first century is a far cry from the tepid content of the last century. It's more animalistic and more debased with each passing decade. And the women on these sites are competing to be the raunchiest, the baddest, the nastiest. If you're on an online dating site, try this experiment: look at a dozen profiles of women in their fifties. Then view a dozen in their forties, then thirties, then twenties. As the age declines, the women are more sexualized. More bi, more "poly," more fetishistic. Try it and see for yourself: start an account on Tinder and select no age prefs. If you're over forty, prepare to be future-shocked.

> *"I eat carbs by day; I eat dick by night."*
>
> *"I will only hold hands until marriage. I will, however, have anal with the right guy."*
>
> TINDER BIOS

Put it this way: How many women over age forty-five have a "sex tape"? How many women younger than thirty-five do? Still not convinced? Many fiftysomething stereotypical single suburban soccer moms (known universally is MILFS) are more tatted/pierced/shaved/trimmed/waxed and more sexually outrageous and adventurous than a 1995 porn star. Believe this. If you're reasonably fit and attractive and over fifty, there is only one clear advantage over a staid and stagnant marriage. The sex you'll be having in the twenty-first century is unlike anything you've known.

On every online dating site in America, women over forty are begging, "Please, if you're young enough to be my son, STOP MESSAGING ME!" In the 1980s, when I was a lad in my twenties, I engaged in a torrid affair with a woman twelve years my senior. At that time, no one, but no one, was dating women more than two or three years older than themselves. That is, until the onslaught of "cougar" porn sites. Or "teacher" porn sites. Or MILF porn sites.

And on and on till the break of dawn.

Porn does to your soul what cigarettes do to your lungs. It infects you, skews your judgment, and warps you. It really does. This is written by someone far from prudish or conservative. I don't need to see any stats on this; I know how my soul feels after viewing.

My soul feels like it needs to wash its hands.

CHAPTER 7
TRAVEL, DAMMIT

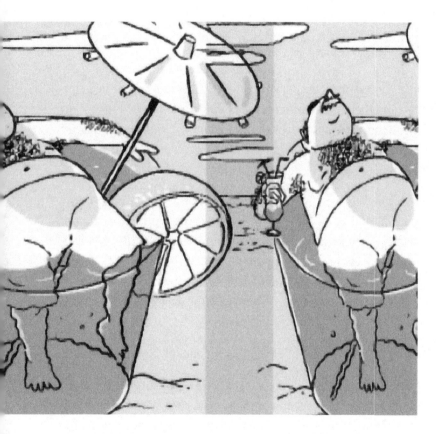

If you're a man over thirty and you don't possess a US passport, I have a serious and sincere question for you:

WTF?

Another:

Really?

You make decent money, you're single, and you're actually thinking of going to Miami with your buds again? Wait, no, it's Vegas? Speaking of Vegas, what are the odds that you'll remember the specifics of your trip? What are the odds of you doing something truly new and different from the last three times you went?

Apply for a damn passport already. It's inexpensive, it lasts ten years, and there is nothing that says you're a citizen of the world like having a passport from your country. No serious, quality woman will date a guy who does not have one. Period and full stop.

Here's an idea: get the passport, go to a travel site (you know the ones), and book a flight to Spain. Make it a long weekend. Book an Airbnb in a cool part of Barcelona, Seville, Madrid, Pamplona, wherever. Bring along a couple of books. That's right, look at fiction and nonfiction bestsellers, do a minute of "research," and buy both. When was the last time you read a book? How about, you know, a novel?

Reading a novel shouldn't be a novel concept. Sorry, I had to.

While in Spain, go to some museums. Big beautiful churches. Have sangria and tapas at a chic outdoor café. Flirt with a local beauty. Take long walks around town late at night. Buy some clothes there, clothes you can't get in the US. Get a radical haircut while you're at it. Live.

For less money than you lost at the strip clubs and gambling tables of Vegas, you'll have come back home a slightly—or not so slightly—different man; a more interesting guy. It's going to whet your appetite for more travel.

Istanbul. Buenos Aires. Bangkok. Vancouver. Ireland. Morocco. Iceland, for Chrissakes.

Just go already. What, exactly, are you waiting for?

CHAPTER 8
THE MANOSPHERE

IT'S TIME TO GO THERE

The flags in this country have sunk almost permanently to half-mast.

No matter what side of the political divide you reside in, it's painfully apparent that we've lost our moorings as a nation. I have a theory, and it goes like this: in any society, a culture rises and falls—for better or worse—on the backs of its men. For *Rampant Douchebaggery* context, I'm relegating white American men to be standard-bearers of this rise-and-fall scenario.

White men have overwhelmingly conducted most of the business and governing of America, and they largely crafted a strong democratic society with an enviable economy. Let's be clear: white American men have created globe-shaking achievements: NASA, baseball, Broadway, the Constitution, Disney, skyscraping architecture and glorious bridges, colleges and universities, Hollywood, Apple; I could go on. Of course, all of this alongside promulgating slavery, breaking treaties, and becoming the face of the modern serial killer, but I digress.

These days, the greatness and the decency mostly appear on grainy black and white film. Look at the news—who has juice? Women are spacewalking while (white) men are being arrested at Walmart with a cache of assault weapons in their trunk.

Who is making bold moves? Who is taking courageous action in our government and society? Lots and lots of energized and empowered women of all stripes—gay, straight, young, not so young, Muslim, Jew, and Catholic alike—are taking power, real power, into their own hands.

So many men are not happy about this.

Something about the internet, men, and decency doesn't jibe. That's a central theme. RD has taken a few twists since I began this project. It has largely avoided politics. However, the book you're now reading has also skirted a growing issue, a veritable epidemic among single white men in America:

A decade old movement that's been mushrooming in the dank basement apartment of the almost more bad than good internet. It's known as the Manosphere.

You've no doubt heard of the website Reddit? Or Reddit sub-threads? Ever hear of Epik? 8kun? (These change like the seasons, btw.) Hoo boy. Here we go.

For young men who've grown up hypnotically staring at small screens for most of the hours of most of the days of their lives, the present and future are kinda grim. Beginning with Game Boy, growing into WWE, UFC, then by, say, age ten or eleven, binging on Fortnite and other addictive and unhealthy gaming platforms, while simultaneously descending into the mire of modern porn—nasty, thrilling, vulgar, degrading, racist modern porn—until finally sinking into YouTube and Reddit, etcetera, describes a downward spiral that we've kept hidden, that we've normalized. Any examination of the core culture of gaming, WWE/UFC wrestling, sports radio, and porn will yield galaxies filled with and fueled by racism and misogyny.

Growing exponentially, domestic terrorism in America is over-whelmingly right wing. If we erase from the frame or make blurry the hands on father—and where the mom is less educated and socially liberal—we're looking at a young fearageous white man whose view of the world can, and often does, look like this:

At one end of the spectrum, there are MRAs (men's rights activists), who ostensibly "educate" men about the perils of vicious and crazy wives, or soon to be ex-wives. Though their mission is purportedly to ensure that men are not "victimized" by women using the legal system, the culture is a petri dish of misogyny and fear. Women are almost always viewed as crazy bitches seeking to rob men of their self-worth and hard-earned wages, leaving them penniless and broken.

But wait: How many women have been accused of committing "revenge porn"? (In July of 2020, one of these MRA losers shot a "feminazi" judge's son and husband. White American men and guns often go together like baking soda and vinegar.)

Female readers may not be familiar with sports talk radio. This is an AM/FM radio version of the online culture: poor to moderately educated white men with time on their hands, who appreciate Black or Brown men when they're entertaining us on the court or the stage, fanboys who think "chicks" and "psycho bitches" should shut the freak up and stop getting in the way.

As we peer into the sordid, racist, violent, and misogynistic netherworld of online gaming—a world that, like sports radio, WWE wrestling, and porn, is dominated by hostile, unsocialized white guys—we've discovered far too late this fearful, isolated, and anger based culture has full on embraced the fascistic, racist, and misogynistic Donald J. Trump. And an alt-right ecosystem that is kind of, you know, white supremacisty. These same guys might automatically view me, in turn as an "SJW" (social justice warrior) or "snowflake" or whatever, but nope.

Pornhub, the Amazon of online pornography, sells Trump coins.

They do not sell Biden coins, let alone Hillary coins.

Trump is an avowed "pussy grabber" and amoral racist. His alter ego, Steve Bannon, popularized the term *cuckservative*. What's a *cuckservative?* Its origin lies in porn. In porn, a cuck is mainly a weak white guy who, because of his weakness, is forced to watch his hot wife have brutal sex with a Black man, known on porn by these nonhuman descriptors: Bull. Monster. Savage. Beast.

On the more extreme part of (insert website of the moment) in Internet Town, this confused and isolated culture contains less rational types:

- Chads (dudes who always get laid)
- Alphas (same)
- Betas (weak weak weak)
- Staceys (who choose to bed down only with Chads—but not with inccls)
- Incels (as in involuntarily celibate)

Incels are grown men who claim that due to their lack of mojo, bad looks, and unsocialized manner they're completely frozen out of this world of crazy limitless sex with the Staceys, who are avatars for the illusory porn stars they love/hate. Two—wait, make that three—such man-boys have killed multiple people in attacks in the past two years.

Because they were not getting laid.

Are you ready for this? On 4chan/8kun, there are message threads where isolated white male posters encourage other isolated white men into "going through with" plans to shoot up a school or theater. This is actually happening right now, today in the spiritually ill USA. This is a new breed of white guy; the only true philosophy he hews to is nihilism. The misplaced fury, the armchair vigilante's need to avenge speaks to an angry everyman, in turn egged on by a growing grievance media complex that feeds and despises viewers in equal measure. Outside of a Klan leader, this guy never had a voice in the past. The KKK used to be fringe. According to the Southern Poverty Law Center tracking these trends, hate groups are up, up, and away from the numbers of yesterday.

When you think of a "hate group" today, what demographic comes to mind?

At the end of the day, we all seek the same thing: connection, a desire to belong to something or someone. For a mounting number of men, fear, isolation, and a lack of kind, compassionate role models are virtually crushing any chance for those same men to rise up in this world and actually be a man. A "community" where you never meet face-to-face, where you know no one's actual identity, is no community at all.

Say what you will about the KKK—at least those fellas know how to socialize.

What's it mean to be a twenty-first-century American man?

American men are anything but standing strong. As the author of this book, I've been guilty of the very thing I'm preaching: A deficit of compassion for my fellow dude. I find so many lacking introspection, lacking curiosity, lacking passion about life itself. I need to go deeper; to see these men as fellow travelers in need of kindness, desperate for direction. Maybe an actual hug from another man. One who doesn't look down on them but instead buoys them up—up into this exciting new world of possibilities, where women are cherished and supported equals. Where the love of nature, of books, of volunteering "just because" are the new normal. Crazy, right?

Real life is just beyond your screen.

Let's turn off. Press the button and shut it down. Take a walk in your neighborhood, talk to a total stranger. Go to your library and pick out a book, any book that feels positive, instead of the opposite. Read it, walk back, return it and repeat.

CHAPTER 9
DOING YOGA WON'T NECESSARILY MAKE YOU GAY*

(*NOT THAT THERE'S ANYTHING WRONG WITH THAT)

Did you know that yoga was invented five thousand years ago by men, for men?

It's high time for yoga to be reassociated with men.

Dudes. Males of the species. Masters of the domain.

Nothing is more beneficial for men as they age than weekly (or daily) yoga.

It's also time for advertisers and those who influence public perception to retire the cliché of the lithesome woman—thin, casually affluent, invariably aged thirty to forty—"doing" yoga as something sorta healthy before latte or lunch with pals. Whenever yoga is shown in a movie, it always serves as a punch line. Goddamn.

I call bullshit on this. OK?

I've been doing yoga for over two decades, and I'll do it until I physically cannot. Why? Because it has transformed my being. Not just my body (which it has), not just my stress levels, not just my sleep, not just my "spirit"—my Whole. Damn. Being.

It's a secret—although it may not be after *Rampant D* soars to the top of the New York Times bestsellers list—that yoga is the Fountain of Youth. For women this is positively true, but I'll argue it's more essential for men.

Think of what we value as men: we want to be able to stand as tall as possible; we want to walk in a manner that's confident, projecting ease and strength in our stride. We want to be more "in control." We want to be able to play sports, make love, master our bellies, and feel younger, no matter if we're thirty or seventy.

Check, check, and check.

One of the few must dos for men is yoga. It's something you can do alone, in a hotel, in jail, or in a comfortable, airy studio space that's well lighted and ventilated and run by nice, competent folks.

Dude, I dare you to walk into the yoga studio in your hood (do two minutes of research: Yelp/Google) and take an introductory or beginner class. Buy a good quality yoga mat at any Target or Marshalls (a decent one is thirty dollars; an overpriced one is ninety dollars). Wear some decent gear (if you feel like you look pretty good, you won't feel so uncomfortable) and bring a water bottle. That's it, you're ready. Make this investment; it won't go to waste if you won't.

Practicing yoga is exactly what this book is about: an attempt to get American men of a certain increasing age bracket to shake off the nonsense that's been foisted about how you should be, should act, should . . . forget "should." It's not a word that should exist in your vocab.

Like getting a passport, or having a suit tailored from scratch, or taking a long weekend trip by yourself to a place you've never been, practicing yoga regularly is a game changer that will have you walking a bit more upright. But it takes courage, real courage, to tell your buddies you're now a yogi. Guess what? They'll secretly be envious when they see the steady transformation you're undergoing.

The bennies:

- Strong core, meaning less back pain.
- Better sleep.
- Improved posture.
- Better sex life.
- Increased mental focus.
- Classes where you'll likely be surrounded by fit women in snug clothing.

- Better digestion and, um, elimination. Yep.
- More damn flexible. Like deeply flexible. Stop pretending that being stiff is "how guys are."
- More energy and yet . . .
- More deeply relaxed.
- Better sex life, again.

What are your excuses for not trying this for a month of your life? Three times a week for ONE MONTH. You tell me. If you don't feel different in all aspects of your being, I'll return the price of this book.

CHAPTER 10

DUDE, A

WHY ARE MEN SO FRIGHTENED OF
A SPECIES THAT VIEWS PARALLEL
PARKING AS AN ELUSIVE SKILL?

YOU'RE COWARD

Let's get real. The weekly Walmart shootings, the theater shootings, the school shootings, the church shootings, the festival shootings are killing more than just the intended targets.

It's killing and crushing the soul of this once (relatively) safe nation. Men—white men, angry men, right wing men—are numbingly almost always the culprits. That's largely due to men's fear, paranoia, rage, and self-isolation. Oh, that last one.

Blow up anything you term a *"cave."* American men are repressed, by and large, in ways women are not. And women are oppressed in ways men are not. Huh.

Consider: 60 percent of marriages end badly.

And who is actually saying, "Enough!"?

Eighty percent of the time it's women.

Most men are going to hate hearing this. No one likes to be called out, especially on subjects that are so close to the bone.

But the sad truth is that most dudes are 100 percent scared shit-less by some stuff.

Like what?

- Smart, self sufficient sexy women, for starters, especially if she's better paid, traveled, and educated.
- Visiting a doctor of any kind, especially a therapist or counselor, as in psychologist. This one is uncommonly common among men. How many male partners refuse to see a counselor while in a troubled relationship?
- Being alone/wanting to only be alone. Males and females share the former, but it's typically men who seek the latter. Often this can lead to destruction of lives, families, and communities—more half-mast flags. Loads of men are terrified of solitude or introspection of any kind, and perhaps that's where the problem lies. Fear of feelings. The paralyzing inability to ask for help.

- Living. Suicide rates for white men in America are swept under the rug. This is yet another national tragedy. Approximately 126 Americans die by their own hand each and every desperate day in the US. Nearly 101 of these—the largest demographic by far—are white middle-aged men.
- Looking inward, and of "change."
- Showing emotions. Relative to women, why does it seem that men might take more risks financially or physically, but not emotionally?
- Being intimate. Many men live in a fear cave that women have no clue about. Please read that sentence a few more times. Ladies, you may think that your last man was/is often frightened in odd ways, but most guys are as well.

I've noticed, in my research, a troubling thing: married women rarely, either online or in person, position themselves as single. But married guys do that. A lot. Why is such an elemental example of personal ethics being kicked in the face? Why is it that, in general, men are less trustworthy than their female counterparts? So much creepier? Not only are wives frequently erased from the picture, so are the kiddos in many instances. Maybe I'm warm and fuzzily romantic, but were American men always so skeevy? The answer is a hard no.

I was around in the sixties and seventies. I was born in the goddamn 1950s. Men were more decent to others, more polite, demonstrably less douchey. And, generally speaking they dressed better.

Let's assume I've had five hundred dates from online dating sites. Of these five hundred, how many of these women got too drunk on our date? How many showed up surprisingly bald? How many women misrepresented themselves regarding living arrangements? In five hundred dates, I can count on one hand—fine, make it two hands—the ladies who were guilty of real, deep deception. Based on the hundreds of women interviewed for this book, the percentages of deceptions such as these are nearly the opposite for men. (However, when confronted with the notion that many men are deceptive / cray cray, it's always surprising how many women say, "Oh, but women are just as bad." Nope, they're not.)

Fellas, if you're single and over thirty, you might find that whole living alone thing a bit of a drag. You should keep in mind one simple truth: most gals aren't overly concerned about how much you earn or how hot you look.

There are, of course, thousands of women who do demand a maximal bread earner, as well as a hottie who can make them feel naughty.

But you know what? If you cherish and make your woman feel safe, she'll repay it a thousandfold. Women want and need, above all else, a man they can trust and admire, really admire. That's it. Do what you say you will do. Say what you mean; mean what you say. In short, respect yourself and show this in measurable ways:

Get your damn teeth fixed.

Start to work on your body. Nothing will improve your sense of confidence so profoundly as being very, very fit. Very fit is very hot, even more so as you age. Women love this more than you know.

Don't wear the same clothes as your stepson. The latter years of the 1960s completely shredded men's fashion sense in the US. Why is it OK to go to an upscale restaurant wearing cargo shorts and flip-flops with a tank top or ratty T-shirt? (And we wonder why so many American men are mired in this Peter Pan syndrome?)

After the age of thirty, a man should look like a man, not a boy. Buy some decent shoes and shirts, for God's sake. I dare you to wear a suit jacket out to a nice joint. Double dare you. And please take off that baseball cap.

Here is where the fear thing comes into play. It's as old as Moses; we're afraid of being ridiculed or sticking out. In short, women are afraid of women's disapproval, and likewise for men. What if it were the other way around? What if we weren't so fearful of what others thought?

Attend events and join groups/meetups that have nothing to do with beer, gambling, nudity, sports, or work. This one may be hard. Perhaps the most profound distinction between men and women in the present culture is that women are outward-bound, and men are inward-bound. Again, look at any café or bistro in any town in the US on a Thursday night: you will see table after table of women making small talk or not, having a good time with their gal pals or not, wondering where the great guys are. Or not. Where, in fact, are the guys on that night? Sports and porn might be the most likely caves into which the search committee might shine a light.

This book challenges you, dude, to traverse *terra incognita*. Look it up.

Looking it up is the part I want to impress upon you. Wake up and get curious! Be curious about any damn thing that does not involve what you already know too much about.

In modern America, men are too focused on too few things.

Last, seek assistance on what you most think you need some help with. If you need help with fitness, get a cool personal trainer, maybe of the opposite sex, but don't hit on her. Instead, pick her brain. Work your ass off with intention, self-respect, and sublime, steady focus. Trust me, you'll get feedback that will show you that you've stumbled onto something good. If you need help with fashion, see a tailor or go to a few upscale clothiers. They'll set you straight, my friend.

But if you need help with relationships—all manners of human relationships—see a really good therapist. If Tony Soprano could do it, you can too.

CHAPTER 11
ET TU,

VIRAL DANCE CRAZE,
EVERYONE'S DOING
THE NARCISSIST

CHICK?

"My ex is a total narcissist."

If I received $1.50 each time I've heard this, I'd be a billionaire. The guy you walked down the aisle with was once that swaggery fella, chock-full of all that confidence you say you adore so much. If you like "a guy that's a bit cocky," why are you surprised the cock part became dominant? Why are we surprised this chrysalis turned a cocky caterpillar into a butterfly of a narcissist?

At this point in the story, we turn our gaze to the opposite sex. This primer depicts the various ways the menfolk have complicated things; let's have a look-see at what women may be contributing to the mix.

Simply put, women give dudes too many passes. From loving the bad boy—so pervasive as to be cliché—to ignoring massive red flags (Did he get wasted on the first date? Ask you about sex a lot? Talk a bit too much about his horrible ex?) to allowing boorish behavior to flourish ("I'm sort of a big deal") women may often be complicit, or tacitly condoning. For these behaviors to mitigate, women must wage a united front, *a va-jay-jay vigilance* against douchebaggery.

Lysistrata, a Greek play from 411 BC, held the position that women could influence men to not wage war by withholding sex. Whoa! Hold up. Let's not be rash here. Sex is something most of us appreciate. A lot. But if one in three women sleep with men on the first date (a statistic that has not changed percentages over the past ten years) it can explain—as opposed to excuse—why some men seem to feel this whole online dating is shopping for candy of the carnal variety. Sex is something that, as adults, of course, we can engage in whenever it's mutually desirable. But if we agree with the statement, "The easier it is to find sex, the harder it is to find love," then is it too simplistic to suggest that maybe, just maybe, waiting at least a little while before coitusing can't hurt, and might even help both parties make a better decision?

Everyone's a little insecure, and innate human insecurity generally makes the world go 'round. Online dating can make you feel insecure, and the notion that a guy might not stick around if the female makes it difficult for him is not uncommon when there are dozens of other choices a click away.

Bullshit. After reading literally thousands of online dating profiles posted by women mid-thirties to mid-fifties, I feel certain that women who have standards in place, and maintain that focus, will not accept . . .

- "Hey, what's up?" for an introductory note.
- "Netflix and chill" for an early date.
- A man unwilling to drive or Uber to the woman's home and pick her up for future dates.
- Sharing your number or talking before actually writing informative messages/texts to establish a sense of the writer.
- Responding to a man who shares little info.

I could go on, trust me.

Women have no idea of their power. If women collectively raised the bar on acceptable behavior from their men, like actually expecting a gentleman to pick them up with a plan for the evening and to move the ball safely down the field of play in their relationship, this world would be a smoother ride. And that same expectation holds that a well groomed non-intoxicated on time gentleman could reasonably transition into a worthy husband and father.

Please don't tell me the notion of a man courting a woman is dead and done.

Ladies, it is if you let it. I'm reminded of an old axiom: we teach people how to treat us.

Consider:

- If a man is a lout and has no drive in life, no real passion for living fully in this world of ours, move on.
- If the guy you date is deeply cynical about important things like love and marriage and the state of the world, let him fester on his own.
- If the guy you're with lets you do most of the decision making—and spending—take a pass on him.
- If he never surprises you with actual kindness, let go of him. If his friends are not those whom you'd be friends with on your own, take a moment.
- If he's more interested in making you interested in him than in being interested in you, step away.
- Is he humble? Come on, be honest. Never underestimate the pervasiveness of narcissism.
- Does he laugh at himself? Is he forgiving when you mess up?
- Does he have dreams? Is he working realistically toward them?
- What is his attitude toward his work? Just a gig? Is there a sense of balance between work and play?
- Does he help others, especially those he doesn't know?
- Is he curious about the world around him?
- Does he "show up"? Or, another way of saying this...
- Does he do what he says he'll do?
- Does he put your stuff—you know, feelings, needs, concerns, like that—ahead of his?
- How is his relationship with his own mom and dad?
- Is he honest?

It's shocking how many women have let bad behavior, douchey attitudes, lack of curiosity, substance abuse, anger issues, and narcissism into their lives, sometimes for decades.

Why is this? Miss, if your dad was sort of a dick, why would you want to marry or date a guy Just. Like. Him? How'd that work out for your mom?

On a personal level, I've been on far too many dates with American women. I've run the gamut of experiences, from mildly confusing to pleasantly boring to *"Check, please!"*

There's a question I've asked a few women more than once, as I slowly became aware of the hot mess I found myself chatting with:

"If you found a really good man, would you know what to do with him?"

CHAPTER 12
BOYZ II MEN

"It's easier to build strong children than to repair broken men."

FREDERICK DOUGLAS

When did it become a given that a white American dude must be a num-nut? When did American men stop resembling their grandfathers?

It's time to pause whatever we're doing as teachers, parents, and mentors and get real about how young men are being raised in these swift times.

There's obviously been a profound evolution of the culture from the days when I was in high school. There simply was no common platform for young teens to escape from parents' control. By contrast, today there's no control over anything considered "private." As we sink into the twenty-first century, men in America are growing up in a more porn-fueled, gamed-out, texted- and sexted-up culture where things come easy and reward is expected, especially for young heterosexual white men. The rite of passage of getting that first job has been delayed—let's admit, policy-wise, boomers have not helped the youngins—and the culture of fanboys, of bros, of slackers, of gamers, of budding douches-to-be resides in fertile soil.

Concurrently, sex has been morphing into a more porn-centric pastime—lovemaking is quaint and done for. Where once couples may have fumbled around, now girls and boys could essentially YouTube any manner of sex act imaginable and see how the pros do it. Sex has become performative. More about power exchanges. Fetishes flourish.

Into this mad new world—where it's not unheard of for a stereotypic PTA mom, or high school teacher, to seduce a teenage boy; where "barely legal" porn sites compete with MILF and cougar sites; where gangbanging has become a known quantity—walks a young man. And if his dad is MIA financially, emotionally, and spiritually, this young man, in a shifting and confusing environment, has barely a prayer to be the one to say, "Stop it, that's not cool," when the night turns.

Male bullying, sloppy creepy frat houses, male athletes, male soldiers, male gamers, male bosses—men who are drunk with power and privilege, if not booze—the lot of it needs a total and complete reboot. I'm absolutely sick beyond the pale of reading of frat house rape. Of rape in the barracks. Of rape on the playgrounds and campuses. This is what we're up against as a society: a banner proudly unfurled on one of America's toxic frat houses reads,

- *"No means Yes, and Yes means Anal."* Let that sink in.

Another banner, proudly displayed by yet another frat house for all to see as the school year begins:

"Thanks, Dad, for dropping off your daughter. Mom, you're hot too."

That's as repugnant as it is menacing; yeah, pun intended.

This is an epidemic, and your son or nephew or little bro is culpable. We need to talk.

The fear that men carry concealed like a starter tattoo is so insidious, so pervasive, so stealthy, it's truly a virus. Good men, and those about to enter manhood, are afraid. Afraid of being called the worst thing a heterosexual American male can be called:

a pussy.

Simply slinging that word freely as the ultimate slur is at the root of the problem.

Let me explain. That vile P-word is of course slang for female genitalia. It's also been synonymous with weakness in men for ages, at least in modern American culture.

So take a word that has to do with the most innately female anatomy, and marry that to a code for weakness, and *voilà*, you get misogyny and bullying all at once. One stop shopping for any douche. Men, young men especially, need counsel and good models and courage. The courage to defend. The courage to not fit in with assholes.

How did we get this far down the damn rabbit hole? When did slipping someone's daughter roofies, a date rape drug, become a thing among young men? When did it become the new normal for a nineteen-year-old man-child to pose as a thirty-two-year-old man-child in order to troll a forty-eight-year-old woman for sex online?

We're witnessing a whole new species of American manhood.

Consider this: literally thousands of Uber and Lyft drivers have been accused of assaulting their (mostly female) passengers. How come that didn't seem to be a thing when all those yellow cabs picked us up in the twentieth century?

Q: How many women have ever placed a hidden camera in the men's room?

If your son or brother is addicted to small screens for his entertainment, beware. That little screen is a delivery system for all sorts of shit, like violent and misogynist videos. Like porn that's all about power and degradation as opposed to traditional (vanilla?) sexual interaction. Like whack WWE and UFC wrestling/fighting that's simply toxic to a young man's brain. Add in the too busy or barely there dad, and that young man has a terrific chance of becoming yet another fearful, repressed, and pissed-off bad guy.

Include to the mix young women eager to play their often complicit new role in this American tragedy, and our butts are sliding on butter down that rabbit hole.

The thought that your son or little bro might be a bad guy is chilling, yes?

CHAPTER 13

MISANDRY

GIRL VS GIRL

VS MISOGYNY

Most of you already know one of the two title words.
The other? Not so much.

Misogyny is defined as "contempt for women." Misandry? My spell-check alerts me that I must mean missionary? Or perhaps *milady*? Who knew milady was still so *en vogue*?

Misandry is contempt for men. The fact that neither I nor anyone in the universe knows the definition of this word—from female academics to the staff at a legendary feminist bookstore—is telling. How is it that most of us know only one version of gender contempt but not the other?

Two likely answers: contempt for women is much more prevalent, and more violent, than the other scenario, and women have done a more thorough job of politicizing the contempt concept.

Ready? Overwhelmingly the most gleeful and spirited contempt for women that I have personally experienced comes from women themselves.

I'm referring to the dozens upon dozens of times I've heard women—with glee—use the term psycho bitch to talk about another woman. Or, after having related an anecdote about a legitimately cuckoo female to another female acquaintance of mine, how often (and again, with real zest) that woman will excitedly ask if I've heard from/seen "that crazy psycho bitch"? Or this: an acronym, "RBF," refers to a *resting bitch face*. Any bets on which gender employs that term of misogyny most frequently, if not exclusively? Why did so many women possess a white hot loathing for Hillary Clinton?

Why are so many women contemptuous of other women?

Why aren't they more contemptuous of men, who are far more contemptible than most women could ever be?

A conundrum, yes? And for the men? Do they possess the same negative zeal for other men as many women have for their "sisters"?

The answer is a resounding "No." And that's a problem. Men don't police other men the way women do to each other. Notice I said "to" as opposed to "for." Women "policing" each other feels tribal and very limiting. In fact, much of that policing is essentially slut shaming of varying degrees.

For example: Evanston, Illinois, is a liberal, educated suburb north of Chicago, home to Northwestern University. You'll be hard pressed to find many women walking the streets there in stilettos. It just isn't done. The slut shaming whisper campaign would put an end to that.

Men could give a rat's ass about that, by and large. The following are the only things that matter to most guys about other guys: How much do you make, and how hot is your babe? That's as pathetic as it is accurate. Of course, you must conform to some degree. If you're too metro, no good. Too hippieish, same. Beyond that, guys simply don't care about other guys in that way.

So, then, how will this book resonate with its subjects? How will men take to being told they might want to shape up, become a bit more self-aware? Perhaps they'll say, "You know what? I could lose that gut and maybe buy a suit. Work out a bit. Maybe even get one of those passports that guy was talking about . . ."

Yet God forbid American men be told they need, just a tiny bit, to "get in touch with their feminine side," or torrents of testosterone will burst the dam. That's almost like saying American men might be well served to take a page out of their northern neighbors' book and become just a bit more like our Canadian brothers: polite, nondouchey, nonaggressive. And, again, super polite.

And most US males' response to that? Perhaps something along the lines of "kiss my ass." American men, especially those born in the twentieth century, have been raised to be the "rugged individual" like, yes, John Wayne, to use the most tired cliché of all. Yet how about Mark Wahlberg's bad boy heroes? Or Clint "Feeling lucky, punk?" Eastwood? Or perhaps Donald Trump? Of the four male icons mentioned, how many are frankly assholes? Hint: not the Duke; the old-school tough guy persona didn't necessarily imply a lack of decency. This is the thesis.

Why do we call men "successful" when they merely make money? In fact, I'll posit that many "successful" (i.e., high salaried) men are complete, unreconstructed assbags.

If women stalked, sulked, preened, bullied, drank, cheated, and lied with as much impunity as these "high powered" men, this world would spin in the opposite direction, leading to planetary ruin. Catastrophe on a biblical scale. Yet it never ceases to amaze me that women give these men, these frankly overly entitled man-boys, a 100 percent pass. In the same way that there's no male equivalent for "slut," there is no male equivalent for "*psycho bitch.*" Or even just "psycho." Or "bitch" itself, for that matter. Again, DJ Trump.

In America, "strong" is usually crisscrossed with aggressive. A man, especially if he's white, can be beloved as a curmudgeon. That is to say, an asshole of sorts. Think Tucker Carlson, Joe Rogan, David Letterman, Alec Baldwin, Bill O'Reilly. Why is that? Black men cannot be curmudgeonly (google Bill Cosby; wait, don't, after all). Nor can women, lest they be accused of being "hormonal." And there you go: misogyny by men against women who have a strong voice, which is like always: see Jane Fonda, Whoopi Goldberg, Megan Rapinoe and Gloria Steinem, if any guy knew or cared who she is.

To be a douche, you must by definition be privileged. Hence, in America, white and male.

Women in the West, especially in America, are gaining visibility and actual power in modern society. Is it fair to say that along with a rise in visibility on the world stage an even harsher, greater torrent of abuse and terror has arisen? Or is it just an example of an increase in the means to inflict, measure, and monitor this misogyny?

Let's tally up: women are quite possibly the most misogynistic. Too many men are very misogynistic, yet not very misandrist. And women are not very misandrist at all. Except, politically speaking, on the far left of the spectrum. You may disagree, but you may be wrong. Conservative women tend to be sharply misogynistic but are blindly patriarchal, while liberal women tend to be majorly in love with their fellow sisters of all stripes (especially the educated ones). Yet these "lefty" progressive sistas are solidly anti-patriarchy. Our left/right, liberal/Republican brains are wired very differently.

Why can't contemporary men and women, navigating life as well as any of us mortals can, just root for each other? And perhaps serve and protect each other?

CHAPTER 14

THE CASE FOR

VOLUNTEERING

Unlike women, who are survival oriented and inherently more social beings, most men are stuck inside their own world.

We jokingly refer to a "man cave," but it's not a damn joke. Men need to bust out of all caves and burst into the sunlight.

One of the best ways to go about this is to volunteer. At least a little bit.

Volunteering, like eating right, doing yoga, or meditating, has unfortunately become a "chick thing." That's one of the reasons I'm writing this book. We need to create new paradigms, ones that make the above, but especially volunteering, "cool" for men. When we think of someone "doing volunteer work," does anyone picture a man? Of course not. This is ridiculous and must be changed if men are to leave the twentieth century behind.

Let me relate from my own experience. I've done a bit of volunteering in a few disparate areas, and all of them were worth my time and effort. I donated my lunch hours back when I was in an office environment and would go to an organization in Chicago called Jobs for Youth, a wonderful nonprofit that helps inner city kids get a leg up on a potential career. My role was to meet with young men and women and help them craft a résumé. The kids were eager and motivated. To a person they took direction and came back correct. At the end of the semester there would be a small party for the young men and women, who were full of hope and optimism. To be thanked for doing a small deed is like being kissed on the cheek of your soul.

The most surprising aspect of this experience? It was liberating myself from my office, my space, my head, my skinny world of privilege.

I've since donated my time to other pursuits, such as mentoring young men from the city. Again, to have impacted a "stranger" in a positive way, while seeing how other people, wholly different from you, live and think is a gift in and of itself.

I had always wanted to volunteer for Habitat for Humanity. My father was a carpenter, and I was raised with the smell of sawdust, so building a home for a deserving family was deeply resonant. I had also developed a mad love affair with the city of New Orleans. When Hurricane Katrina hit the Gulf in 2005, I felt as though I had been kicked in the gut. I vowed to myself and to my friends that I would go down there and help in some way.

Months passed. One day I was perusing the interweb and came across a site for NOLA (New Orleans, Louisiana) Habitat for Humanity. Oh. I knew I could not click away from this one.

With a gulp, I signed up for a stint (they let you work in three day shifts). It happened to coincide with the New Orleans Jazz Fest, because, why not, right?

I traveled south from Chicago to New Orleans, going the opposite route of Louis Armstrong in the 1920s. I arrived during a torrential storm that was a true squall, biblical in its scope and fury. I didn't want to be stuck for even a day in a hotel room. I found my way to the apocalyptic Ninth Ward site of the Musicians' Village and waited and waited for them to allow us to work, mud or no mud. Then the sun eased out.

I was so pumped to work, I gladly spent the rest of the day piling sand into a wheelbarrow, dumping it out twenty yards away and repeating. For seven or eight hours. No beer in heaven tastes as good as the one you swill after that kind of day's work.

On the second day, the organizers summoned me over and told me they liked my effort and were rewarding me by putting me in a photo op with our forty-third president, George Bush. Now this was interesting. As camera crews documented the prez and me discussing Chicago baseball, we placed tresses on top of brand new above-code homes for struggling musicians. Another night of music, food, and drink in that mysterious town followed by another day of fun: hammering nails and sawing boards for foundations of dream homes.

GWB and JC, in a beer commercial.

I drove back home and realized I'd had the most fun—no, the most *joy*—I'd experienced in ages. Joyful to meet new folks from all over the country. Joyous to do "real" work and sweat. Rewarding to actually get off my behind and do something that means something to someone else.

So much fun that I never made it to my beloved Jazz Fest.

Why do we relegate these three life-changing activities (volunteering, yoga, and reading) to one gender? What about volunteering is so beneficial?

A twentysomething acquaintance had these bennies to offer, without blinking, about volunteering: provides a form of connectedness; exposes you to culture; helps you traverse maturity more easily; keeps you grounded; helps you to have a more positive outlook; helps you to be more secure in yourself; teaches mental and emotional endurance; improves your health (the more active you are, the healthier you are); and provides an opportunity to learn new things.

Well said, and all of it true.

Volunteering expands your horizons, and let's face it, those horizons need some expansion. Unlike women, who are participating in book clubs, attending wine groups, and taking yoga and Pilates classes with coffee or a meal after, men are too often inside and alone, and exhibit zero curiosity about . . . anything much it seems, outside of work and sports and whatever consumes men these days on the small screen. Gaming? Porn? Trolling?

Do some research. Is there anything beyond the screen that holds even a little passion in your life? Like maybe gardening? OK, not a good example. How about pets? Have you ever thought it might be cool to be a Big Brother/mentor to a child who could use it? Can you help someone find and keep a job? Can you offer your time?

I offer this challenge: find a passion, google volunteer opportunities associated with that passion, and have a go. You'll be amazed at how good you feel, like deep down. For men, getting outside of yourself and focusing on something other than you and your job may be the first time you'll experience real joy in ages.

The joy of giving. The joy of helping. The liberation from caveman life. You'll most likely find a whole new perspective on life itself. You've got nothing at all to lose and everything to gain.

And, guys, women adore men who volunteer in earnest.

Isn't it worth a shot?

CHAPTER 15
CHIVALRY IS SEXY AF

Chivalry is a lyrical French word from the late Middle Ages that modern women swoon over and sigh upon hearing, saying typically, "Ah, if only . . ."

Chivalry was initially meant to describe the actions and duties of knights. The concept was a readiness to defend honor, to fight injustice, and to do the small things that make a good man a good man. Simply doing what you say you'll do is practicing chivalry. Standing up for those who are weaker or cannot defend themselves. Speaking up for those who have no voice.

Chivalry is quiet strength. It's the opposite of weakness. The chivalrous are never victims.

I have seen far too many posts from women online that ask, "Are there any good guys left?" Sadly, today many American men are utterly lacking in the chivalry department. Guys by and large don't realize how women crave these ancient manners of manhood. Part of courting, of dating, is showing up. Being a steady, dependable, decent man.

A chivalrous man doesn't talk smack about his friends or exes. He helps out. If men in America today could marshal their best instincts and master the simple art of looking outside of himself, of giving a damn about others, he'd find that women—deep, deep down—melt over this form of decency.

We're not talking about merely opening a car door on a few dates. Chivalry is a lifelong habit of putting others first. In dating, practice the small but important things such as paying for the entire first date. Making sure your date got home safely, perhaps even calling for and paying for an Uber for her.

If you like this woman and respect her as a lady, let her know. Ask her to call or text when she gets home. The very next day, let her know you had a wonderful time and that you want to see her again. Plan date number two and make it better than date number one. Planning is caring. Women are often burned out today because men have left most details of dating up to them.

Think of how relieved and quietly thrilled modern women in America would be after kicking ass at their job, making sure the kiddos are safe and accounted for, knowing that you, their date and perhaps future partner, has got this.

- Chivalry is helping strangers when no one is looking.
- It's helping a friend in need at any hour of the day.
- It's being a great son to your mom or dad as they struggle with aging.
- It's integrity. Integrity married with manners.
- It's knowing when to keep your silence—discretion is the better part of valor—and more importantly, knowing when to speak up.

It's a cocktail of humility and self-awareness that's intoxicating to women, and men who notice.

Chivalry is much more than mere "good manners." It can't be a faked or temporary state.

Try. Open yourself up to brand new and really old concepts. Like chivalry.

CHAPTER 16

A WAY

ED.U.CATE

FORWARD

So many aspects of our American landscape need to be reformed, remade, recontextualized, and deconstructed.

For example, issues such as income inequality, rampant corporate malfeasance, or climate change and fossil fuels. With the exception of climate awareness, education is possibly the most urgent to fix and get right.

Our US educational system, which today is far less influential than the massive apparatus of corporate and social media, is long overdue for a makeover.

I can claim some small authority on this, as I've been in the college or high school classroom for most of my adult life; mostly as an instructor, but also as a student.

For American men to thrive in the twenty-first century, we need to course correct—and in some cases revert back to—modalities of learning that are essential for young men to face a brave newish century.

In the current landscape of US education, young men are behind the eight ball. Punished more, given more meds, dwarfed by more physically and socially evolved girls, outnumbered by females attending and graduating from college, and thoroughly drowning in a female-centric educational system currently at a loss about how to get the most from hyper, hyper, like really hyper young boys. There's no argument that American education is confused. We're miseducating our young men and boys.

Let's get rad. Let's get old school *and* new school.

Broad strokes. Boys might be better served in elementary schools—if not through high school—being taught separately from girls. That's right, and I'm not alone in suggesting this. An all-boys educational system paired with equivalent sister schools for social and cultural events. Boys do much better in the classroom in an environment of minimal distraction. Perhaps better still in an environment of male instructors who are also valued mentors. Incorporate vertical mentors, like high school-ers mentoring junior high boys. College students mentoring HS kids. Like that.

Jesuit schools have a tradition in all-boys education, that of service. They phrase it as Men For Others, and it's an essential component to a learning experience that has literally been around for centuries.

We need to change the perception of being a teacher in America. We tend to almost look down on men who teach any level less than college or university. Yet if we greatly increased the number (and pay scale) for good men to show up and model strong, smart, compassionate maleness, our society would be enhanced. A young man who shows up every day, ready to lead, having had amazing mentors, prepping to be a mentor himself, challenging and embracing progressive and time-honored learning concepts throughout American classrooms, would be the soundest and most radical idea of all. Game changer.

What if the challenges and demands of adolescent life were embedded in the curriculum?

It's been shown in recent and multiple tests that boys and girls alike learn better when they can move—physically move around as they learn. So let's do that.

How about making a class that I took as a joke in high school—home economics—mandatory? Along with meditation and yoga, learning to eat, enjoy, and prepare healthy, all-natural food for life is a course correction for men and women. Another class I took that made a huge difference in my later life: consumer education, where I learned about the pitfalls of revolving credit, annuities, and most life insurance. Why not make our citizens better informed consumers, hmm?

Now let's go one better. How about a curriculum that features nature—with an experiential component, even in the city—as an essential element of learning? Learning how to take care of the land, to live off and with the land in ways that are unimaginable today.

How about value-based decision making in real life situations?

Sports. Lots of sports and recreation but not as it's being done today. Not so much an emphasis on "winning" but rather on team building and sportsmanship, authentic and timeless sportsmanship practices that can be used throughout one's life and career.

Yoga in the schools. Yes, this book is written by a yogi, but it's my firm conviction that boys in particular would benefit massively by practicing yoga early and often in their lifetime. This, too, is a game changer, if only we could get over that stupid stereotype of yoga being something "girls do." Why? Yoga has been demonstrated to increase concentration and reduce stress. Yoga shows us that boys and girls can partner and evolve together in a practice that fosters non judgment, patience, and body/mind/spirit awareness. C'mon, it's the twenty-first century already. Let's inaugurate the yoga-in-schools movement and export globally as we have with our cultural exports.

What about sex education/family life?

Sex education refers to "an age-appropriate, culturally relevant approach to teaching about sex and relationships by providing scientifically accurate, realistic, nonjudgmental information" (National Institutes of Health). This definition acknowledges that the aim of sex education extends beyond the transfer of knowledge on human physiology, reproductive system, or the prevention of sexually transmitted infections. Rather, sex education is conceptualized holistically with the goal of empowering youths to better understand their sexuality and relationships, which will ultimately improve adolescents' sexual health and overall quality of life. This is in line with the World Health Organization's delineation of sexual health as "a state of physical, emotional, mental and social well-being in relation to sexuality; it is not merely the absence of disease, dysfunction or infirmity. Sexual health requires a positive and respectful approach to sexuality and sexual relationships, as well as the possibility of having pleasurable and safe sexual experiences, free of coercion, discrimination and violence. For sexual health to be attained and maintained, the sexual rights of all persons must be respected, protected, and fulfilled."

Regarding sex ed, was anyone educated thusly? I know I was not.

This is challenging and necessary. America, in my view, is embarrassingly prudish, still fostering outdated Judeo-Christian puritanical concepts about sex that we carry with us today.

(For example, when we speak of "morality" in the US, it generally refers to sex.)

How about this: Fostering a love for literature and the arts? Crazy, right?

What's crazy is the constant dumbing down of our young men in American elementary and high schools. Why can't young men be exposed to nature, literature, art, and music in a way that feels "male"? Books such as Walden? Knowing and appreciating Henry David Thoreau, John Steinbeck, Ernest Hemingway, Richard Wright, Walt Whitman, Malcolm X—I could go on— books and art tailored to actual boys? As they actually are:

easily bored, legs rattling, needing something or someone to help keep them focused.

Another crazy notion? Civics nerds ruling the schools. Why not? Young men (and women) have little or no idea of our nation's rich history or our branches of government. Nor do they know the true story of our country, in terms of Native Americans, slavery, civil rights, or women's rights. Just saying.

Coding and "twenty-first-century skills" are needed. So is historical context.

How about establishing an incentive to help others less fortunate in the community, or one day cultural exchanges with a slightly distant sister school that would open eyes just by being someplace entirely different for a day or two? This is occurring in a fraction of American schools, yet not nearly enough.

Learning the value of food, nature, money, meditation, teamwork, and self-respect. Respect for women/females; respect for the "other." What a concept.

HIGHER EDUCATION

I'll make this brief, dear reader: humanities—history, philosophy, social sciences, English literature—should not be vanishing from our campuses; they should instead be reimagined and reinvigorated for the twenty-first century. Immersion in humanities actually gives graduates a leg up in many careers. Savvy, forward thinking employers know this and are seeking out English majors. Why? Because this generally means an employee with better than average speaking, writing, and critical thinking skills. Humanities students have context.

Numerous studies have shown humanities students tend to rise up the ladder when paired with a strong work ethic. If you doubt this, I'm assigning you homework.

Last, let's include foreign exchange, stronger internships, and incentives to civics and volunteering opportunities on campuses.

Civics. Humanities. Volunteering. Sportsmanship. Meditation and yoga. Foreign exchange. Boys-only classrooms. Vertical male mentoring.

Want to see the American man truly become a global force for innovative, enlightened leadership?

CHAPTER 17
I CONFESS, PT. 2

WELCOME TO THE JUNK DRAWER OF MY SOUL

The original title for the first chapter of RD was "Sleepwalking with a Boner." That title was descriptive of my lack of awareness in life and love. I had no idea.

I've been the proverbial "late bloomer," or if you prefer to go snarky, an exemplar of the Peter Pan syndrome. As a kid on the South Side of Chicago, I was terribly naive and terrifically sheltered from how the world worked for others less fortunate. We were far from well off yet had all the creature comforts a middle class existence affords.

I had no idea—in truth, until the 2014 protests in Ferguson, Missouri—how privileged I was (and am) as a white, heterosexual, Christian-ish male. The first time I was aware of any "persecution" toward my way of life was when as a late teen I discovered that nasty folks like the KKK had a thing against Catholics, a crew I most definitely belonged to at that time. I was shocked that anyone could be against—as in to destroy—a way of life, a culture, I took for granted.

Things went my way, mostly. I was successful in school, at sports, and in friendships with both boys and girls. My neighborhood went from all white to virtually all Black in the blink of an eye—two quick-morphing years. My friends were Black, and that was the first time I witnessed that stereotypes were often inaccurate. My Black friends were nerds and were not too different from me, except they didn't get spanked—they got *"whupped."*

I remain grateful to this day that I had this life lesson in cultural awareness at such a formative time. Once, my Black friends and I got on a bus that was all Black. The others on the bus started yelling, *"Honky, get off this damn bus!"* It was a vocal inferno. Without batting an eye, my Black friends got off the damn bus with me. Because of this and many more experiences, I never demonized nor romanticized Black men. What I did not do was truly empathize with how radically different their circumstances and experiences could be from mine on a day to day basis. And not only were Black men excluded from my myopic worldview: LGBTQ, Latinos, women—anyone that wasn't me had a trickier road to traverse.

I went through life expecting things would go my way forever and ever. I never had to fear. Never had to duck or hide from anything or anyone—I was a white hetero christian male in America. Until things just didn't work. I had been in failed relationship after failed relationship. I thought women were mostly goofy and manipulative creatures. I was vain, clueless, and unhumble. I came to a brick wall, and I asked for help.

For me, therapy was a two year epiphany. I was humbled for the first time as a grown man. I made changes as a result that enabled me to grow immensely and to help others too.

Then I dipped my toes into the choppy waters of online dating, something that was stigmatized by many folks in the early 2000s.

Here's where it gets pathetic.

I once attempted a short book-to-be, entitled *Mitch.Com*—get it? Mitch, as in Match? Ugh. "Mitch" was me. I wrote episode after bewildered episode until . . . until I couldn't take any more of it. I had written a fairly straight-up account of several dates. Midwestern women, all single or divorced, late thirties to fifties in age. And the result was sadder than I would've guessed. A lot of hurt, a lot of scars, unable or unwilling or unknowing how to heal. How to trust. How to not be ridiculously busybusybusy.

(Online dating can be a cornucopia of assumptions, a hothouse of deceptions, a funky gumbo of jaundice, self-delusion, rage, abject confusion, fear, and chronic frustration. Enjoy!)

My journey is far from over, and I've got more to learn, but I know this—gratitude is essential for human growth and well-being. And if you extend a hand, forward or behind you, someone you least expect will be there to take it.

CHAPTER 18
THE DOUCHISSIST

IT'S CALLED WINNING

There's a particular strain of American male, and he's using up too much of our oxygen.

You've seen him in the arena, in the courtroom, on TV, and in film. You've experienced him having "road rage"; you've spied him in the comments section of online blogs, telling total strangers how stupid and ugly they are; or perhaps he's strutting on the floor of the stock exchange. He is the douche/narcissist; or, for brevity:

the Douchissist.

White American men have held the spotlight as the rugged cowboy individualist blah blah blah for so long that it's sort of understandable if they feel a right to own their swagger. And it's equally comprehensible that these same men might feel a bit piqued when the earth shifts perceptibly under their wing tips and loafers.

Swagger is not the issue. Real swag is always welcome if it's authentic, because most of us are attracted to confidence, inner drive, and fire in the belly. That's not what this chapter is about. It's about a man who is exponentially common in the US today—the narcissist who is also an unkind douche of a man. The defining, distinctive birdcall that exemplifies this man? *"I'm sort of a big deal."*

This man has lurked around the fringes of America for decades, of course, and he's not unique to the States either. Yet this dude, this ego-fueled, ungracious, non-humble, non-introspective man who believes he is simply more important than others, portends a troubling trend in our culture.

The phrase *"toxic masculinity"* has become a thing. It's a "thing" due to the troubling rise in douchiness in American men. Examples from American culture abound. Think of Joe Rogan, Matt Lauer, Elon Musk.

Or, Chevy Chase, Mel Gibson, Alec Baldwin, Steven Seagal, Mark Wahlberg, Kevin Spacey, Shia LeBouf, Bruce Willis, Vin Diesel, Ezra Miller, James Franco, Jared Letto (OK, actually most white male movie stars today); Olympic swimmer Ryan Lochte, former pitcher Roger Clemens, Lance Armstrong, Baker Mayfield, Brett Farve, Aaron Rogers, and yep, even Tom Brady (OK, actually most successful white male athletes); Bill O'Reilly, Sean Hannity, Rush Limbaugh, Tucker Carlson, Alex Jones, Greg Gutfeld, Jesse Watters, Jim Jordan, and Matt Gaetz (or as hot congresswoman Nancy Mace said in 2023, "republican men need to stop being assholes to women.")

Think of a guy who is a bully. Who preens. A man who has no idea how privileged he is. A man who doesn't know the concept of the double standard. This same man is the first to cry "foul" when things don't go his way.

Quite often this toxic man has had his good fortune handed to him, yet he decries those he feels are getting "handouts."

What makes this faux masculinity so fulsome? So terrifically toxic?

It has to do with the scorched earth nastiness of his persona— casually racist, sexist, and homophobic, while utterly lacking empathy for those who are not him.

This behavior and these beliefs are all the more glaring today in the face of increased cultural awareness and acceptance. The Douchissist may be a minority, but the megaphone and the cologne make it seem otherwise.

Why has this man become so prevalent?

Why is he so unlike our hardworking, keep-your-head-down-and-work grandfathers?

It's partly due to our collective "dumbing down," but it's more than that. Sad to say, but, character-wise, white American men have lost more than they've gained these past few decades. (Black men in the US historically have experienced too much humiliation, subtle and not so much, at the hands of white dudes to be rendered full-on douche. Repeat: to be a douche in full, you must have experienced a life of privilege.) We've lost our compass, our basic compassionate decency, to a staggering degree.

As mentioned in the first chapter, American men are seemingly less honorable today. Less valorous, less chivalrous. Modern America is a world of instant gratification. It's also a place of desolation, spiritual desolation. Men literally don't do much heavy lifting anymore; we tend to move data around these days, while we're raised less often by men who are present and provide "good modeling." We're more attracted to the vast and murky cesspool of celebrity and pornography than ever. We tend to think—more than ever—that we could be "stars" or "heroes" without making the sacrifice of our time or energy. We're less group social and more self-centered.

And then there is the internet, always giving us what we don't need more of.

We behave the way we think we're supposed to behave. Frat boys think they're expected to be dicks. Frat boys of today would be downright embarrassed if they didn't attend a drunken gangbang in the course of their five year stint.

Of course, the culture at large is not even vaguely the same as it was thirty or forty years ago, as it should be. Yet there is no denying the current American cultural landscape is more violent, more graphically sexual, more vulgar, and more self-obsessed than at any time in the past fifty years.

Culture changes, but modeling and mentoring endure.

Simply put, far too many young men are deprived of the close scrutiny that a hands-on dad can provide. So much of what we learn from our fathers is received through observing: observing how he conducts himself with strangers, with your mom, with your friends, with the waitstaff during dinners out. The lasting effect a good role model imparted may not have been triggered by a wise phrase you had remembered, but rather a lifelong emotional imprint from your close scrutiny of him.

And so, no matter what I write, whatever this book or any other may declare, if you get your life to a place where you're proud of yourself, and if you choose a partner based on character more than cultural references or sexual heat, you stand a good chance to build a life and a home and a family that will stand.

And you, sir, will have the utmost reward: a strong, respectful, compassionate son or daughter who colors you their hero for the ages.

CHAPTER 19

BLACKMAN, YELLOWMAN,

IT'S BEEN A PRIVILEGE

REDMAN, BROWN

The book you're now perusing, written by a privileged white man, has touched on the concept of "reckoning."

And yes, this is reckoning time in America, and by extent, much of the globe.

A core rationale for RD is the idea that all of us need to do—and should do—better in this twenty-first century than we have in the past. We need to be better men, of course, but not only that, we need to be better citizens and neighbors.

By definition, evolving while navigating this journey of life includes expanding our awareness, our consciousness, our sense of fair play and compassion. Is that "woke"?

White American men built historic economies and infrastructure during the nineteen hundreds. Rarely, however, were these men fair with those who were neither white nor men.

The most shameful example of our collective lack of honor is the disgraceful manner in which white men ripped Native Americans from the most beautiful and fertile lands and forcefully moved them to the least habitable places in North America.

Not one single treaty we signed was worth the parchment it was written upon: we reneged on every one. Today, in the richest nation on Earth, we essentially place Native Americans in no-man's-land ghettos, with lots of cruel sunshine to expose a culture gasping from neglect and hopelessness.

Yet we've also neglected—and neglected to acknowledge—the macro and micro sins, crimes of omission, crimes of brutality, crimes of casual business-as-usual systems in which fair play—how we pretend we deal—is promised to and then yanked away from Black Americans, decade after decade. Human beings also forcefully transferred and systematically migrated to other, more "urban" ghettos, with despair and neglect on par with any reservation. In a time of reckoning, we first need to acknowledge. We have consistently and dishonorably cheated and debased, tortured and hazed, an entire culture. Ripped apart families, then blamed the cheated for not being grateful.

Asian Americans are now being harassed, beaten, and even murdered in our cities. Mexican Americans have to bust ass daily to prove they belong.

In my own lily-white enclave, Mexican Americans are welcomed, providing they're holding a leaf blower. Were Mexican Americans to attempt dining in an upscale restaurant, the dagger looks would translate to "Stay in your lane."

It's overwhelming to see people of color in this weary nation rising up and demanding to be heard, to be treated with everyday dignity and fairness. In 2020 good people around the globe responded. For the first time this century, America could claim moral leadership from the streets, from the grassroots of neighborhood and community activists, proud and courageous men and women of color, joined by all types of fed-up and angry citizens of all ages, beliefs, and colors.

And it's not only the color of one's skin. If you're Jewish or Muslim, you're looking over your shoulder right now. Growth is healthy, essential. Weaponizing *woke* shows how dumbed down we've become.

CHAPTER 20
FATHERHOOD

"I hate my ex-wife more than I love my kids."

ANONYMOUS AMERICAN DAD

As the curtain falls, I'm compelled to spill. How do I say this?

I have been given so many gifts, the greatest of them loving, goofy, hardworking parents, and more generous friends than anyone has a right to.

But sheesh. There's a place beyond sad, and you know this.

I spent a life assuming. Judging, expecting, and assuming. The one thing I never thought?

I never thought I would never be a dad.

You see, lots of people love me, a few understand me, but nobody, absofuckinglutely nobody needs me particularly. I'm hero to zero.

All that love ungiven.

If I could hold my daughter as she reads to me, carry her on my shoulders to the farmers' market as she sings a song she just learned. If I could know what it means for just one hour to have my heart swell with molten pride seeing my boy—my boy—as he scoops up a ground ball and throws it to first . . .

And there it is.

I'd weep a fountain if I let myself think on it.

The research I've done for *RD* has broken my heart at times. I never knew. Any dude can be a chucklehead. That's fine. But if you, dude, have been given the greatest gift of all epochs and oceans of time and space—the gift of being a dad—and you abuse that ultimate gift, you do not make time for your name-sake, you abandon or disregard your very blood—then I hope and pray you feel shame sometime soon.

Are you capable of feeling shame? Are we capable of feeling shame anymore? Or is it just another commodity, a card to play when we're busted?

If you only knew how it pierces my heart to hear of a father who's not really a dad. If you only knew how grateful, on a cellular level, I am each and every day for a father and mother who gave everything they knew how to give, then perhaps you might not work so hard at a job that will deaden you. All they want from you, Mr. Dad, is the gift of you. Your precious time. If you take away nothing from this book, please, I beg you, be the goddamn best father that anyone ever had.

Do it for me, a stranger. Do it for all of us out here:

We need you to make that leap from dude to dad.

Take off those blinders and be not afraid—the whole world is waiting on ya.

CHAPTER 21
I CONFESS, PT. 3: #MEFUCKINGTOO

A DOCUDRAMA, IN WHICH NAMES ARE NAMED

Oh the irony. Dear reader, buckle your seat belts.

After therapy, after yoga, in spite of *"the work"* I had put in on transforming myself, I found I was yet again sleepwalking with a boner.

Yes, indeed. Read and weep. Or laugh if you must.

A cautionary tale awaits.

I'd been living in the sticks for a decade. Self exiled from the city of my birth, in a manner of speaking. After a decade of living in a GOP laden crackerville, I was desperate—that's the operative word here—to "get back," get back to where I once belonged.

THE SETUP

I was dating online and came across a woman who was externally gorgeous. Ten years out of therapy, much of which revolved around why I was making bad choices in mates, I allowed myself to get seduced—*"suckered"* is more on point— into engaging with a woman from far away. Self-rendered desperation, being told I was a genius who couldn't be lived without, and pics of a sexy young woman that any hetero man would salivate over made me do what we do when we're not in our right minds: ignore fields of crimson flags. Flags that were hemorrhaging *roja*.

The city I was once at one with loomed foreign and daunting. I had told myself that, to move back to the city, I needed to cohabitate with someone (a female/girlfriend thing) in order to score an affordable one bedroom apartment. Mistake #1.

I flew across country to pick up a woman I knew almost nothing about. Mistake #2. Once I picked her up, we spent a day or so gathering her things and stockpiling them into a rented Ford SUV.

Indeed, red flags were surely raining down on my hiatus from sanity—she'd lived in eight cities in ten years, for example. Her mother, whom she resembled, and did not speak to, was into her fifth marriage. Now, High Maintenance is a condition I'm conversant with. But this was some really high shit: crying, drama with her soon to be ex-roommate, and more crying. When you coo "it's going to be fine" over and over and over, the opposite will occur.

Here is what I told concerned friends: "What's the worst that could happen? I'm not gonna marry her, not going to buy any property with her. It's just a temporary thing."

I was as honorable as I was wise.

We'd spent a fraught week together when I found she was a serial liar. She told me of her two most recent relationships with men—both of whom were abusive. How she had to move—both times—under cover of darkness. With only the clothes on her back. Guns. Mendacity. Fleeing for her life! Twice in a row, back to back.

Fuck me.

I was in the kitchen one night before bed. Her phone was charging, and right there on the kitchen counter, her cell lighted up with a text from her abusive crazy "ex" who was not an ex at all: YOU ARE A FUCKING LIAR was on the screen for me to see. I dove in and saw the thread. Her crazy abusive ex, of whom she feared for her life, was someone she was trying to get back with. OK!

When confronted with this minutes later, she was adroit in dodging and deflecting. Although this was still early stage, I began looking for the exits. And sighing a lot.

Fast forward a month or so. We are now ensconced in a nice one-bedroom apartment in the heart of the city. She's working at a makeup counter; I'm beginning my new career. This is how it felt: like a bad date. Only this bad date continued day after day. We did not belong together, and it was painfully obvious.

For her, this may have been merely another city and another fella from whom she would again have to flee nocturnally. Historically, in the rain.

Our first Valentine's Day was approximately five weeks into our hitch. We'd had a minor dustup over the phone earlier—I wondered why she'd parked my car so far away from civilization. That was it.

When I came home from my gig—teaching yoga at Trump Tower—at 8:00 p.m., awaiting our 9:00 p.m. dinner reservation, the apartment was dark. She was in bed.

Again, 8:00 p.m. I had flowers. Champagne.

Our first Valentine's!

The next morning, we talked. I said, "This is going downhill." She actually agreed with me on something, so there's that. I could see her spinning, and I could see abandonment issues rising up in her Barbie doll eyes and face.

Precisely four days after this sobering evening, she came in the apartment door and proclaimed, "We have to always lock the door to this apartment from now on." (I had been taking the trash out to the hallway's garbage chute and leaving the dead bolt out so that the apartment door would not automatically shut behind me, thus resulting in a fifty dollar unlocking fee.)

She continued: "I just came up the elevator with a gal who told me that some guy burst into her apartment while she was in the shower or something, and it freaks me out."

I was startled to think that this could happen in our nice semi-hipster, semi-affluent high rise on the lake, the one that allowed dogs, where everyone was chatting up cute puppies on the elevator. A friendly place of happy urbanites. I was taken aback, truly shocked that this had occurred right in our building.

She looked at me in an odd way. She later revealed to me that my reaction was too extreme, too over the top. She decided that I was hiding something. That maybe her newest beau was—improbably yet predictably—another dangerous and scary guy.

Life with us listed back and forth, without ballast to shore us up. There simply was no connection or sex or heart-to-heart anything to speak of. I was on a plane with no landing gear, lacking oxygen.

One day, to make her less unhappy, we took a drive up the North Shore of Chicago to the wealthy Waspy environs of manicured lawns and Mexican gardeners and moms at lunch after yoga.

We had about as pleasant a time as we were ever going to have on a gentle, unseasonably warm spring day. We sailed back home to our barely furnished apartment with the deflated inflatable bed, resigned to settle in with the drug of choice, TV, that would stupefy us until slumber.

A knock came on the door. This was a knock that I'll never ever forget, no matter how long I live or addled I may become.

Knocks on doors have their own personality. There is the jaunty rap of the knuckle knock; the demanding knock; the Jehovah's Witness polite knock. This was neither of those.

This was a sickening, evenhanded, expressionless three-beat knock, utterly devoid of any uplift in percussive tone or meter. I actually remember saying to myself, "That's not a good knock; that's a terribly creepy knock. This is not a knock I particularly want to answer."

Yet answer I did.

I opened the door to our apartment, and there stood two beefy, windbreaker-clad men. They asked me if I was me. Warily, I said yes. I asked what this was about. They said, "Let's just go inside."

We moved inside. I asked them once more, "What's this about?"

They told me, "You're under arrest for criminal trespassing."

I was gobsmacked. Knowing I had not trespassed and had no history of such a feat, I stuttered, "How? When? Who? What's going on here? Why can't you tell me any specifics?"

"You need to come with us for processing. You'll be back in a few hours."

Now here is the really creepy part. My troubled GF comes out of the bedroom, clutching her dog, with theatrical Norma Desmond terror in her eyes, and as she looks at me in horror, she is actually leaning away from me as from a leper. That was as shocking to me as the plainclothes cops wanting to take me away without any information about my accuser, or date or location or anything at all.

My head was spinning. I looked at her as you might if you were drowning and she were on a raft. She offered nothing to the cops in my defense.

There is a phrase that literati use to describe a situation such as this: *Kafkaesque* (meaning a circumstance whereby you are accused by "the state" of unspecified crimes). I was never read my rights. With my GF recoiling in horror upstairs—or maybe not—the cops and I rode down the elevator, and as we entered the lobby, in the midst of tapered after work hustle, they put the cuffs on me, hands behind my back, and paraded me through the lobby of my apartment building. I was the "perp," and I was doing the dreaded "perp walk." A real walk of shame. Not a moment I'd ever wish upon you, dear reader.

In the unmarked car, with the nondescript cops in front, me in the back, I was thinking, "Well, this is a story." I still had no idea.

"Why did your girlfriend react that way to you?" one asked me.

"That's a great question" came the reply from the back seat.

We went to the Northwest Side lockup and courthouse, a location once the home of *Riverview*, a legendary amusement park. Nothing too amusing here, I thought.

I was in a holding cell for a few hours (before I was released one cop told me, ("It's taking longer than usual to process you, because you have no record, but it's still searching.")

I took a cab home, and my GF was still up. After ten minutes in the apartment with her I sensed nefariousness. Emanating from her. I left and went up north.

I knew it would take me a while to process this. What you're reading is "processing."

I hired an attorney, but I was still not thinking clearly. She offered to take me on as a client for a one time fee of $4,000. One size fits all: no matter how many appearances, just this one fee.

I should have known, when I told her that the police never read me my rights, and gave me no information whatsoever, and she replied, "I don't go after cops; my father was a cop," that this was not good.

It wasn't.

Exactly one week later, I was in my home in Southern Wisconsin, and it was fifteen before midnight on another quiet, balmy March night, windows open. I heard two men whispering outside my home, "That's his car." . . . WTF?

Suddenly flashlights pierced my bedroom window, and two men were stealthing up my front lawn, fast. Coming just seven days after being taken from my home in handcuffs by two strangers for something I did not do, I viscerally experienced the difference between fear and terror. This would be the latter. I felt as though a hand had literally grabbed my heart and squeezed into a fist.

I staggered to the front door, and the only thing I could utter was, "You have no right to enter my home."

"Do you know Miss X?" one cop asked me.

"Wha? Oh, fuck—is that what this is?"

They came to my home at 11:45 at night to hand me a restraining order from a woman I wish terribly I had never met.

Two weeks later I went with my lawyer—wife of a fireman, daughter of a cop—to deal with this restraining order nuisance. The judge was a no nonsense Irish lady, and she dismantled my ex-girlfriend's "case" for me being a danger to her in five minutes. Flat.

This, however, was the first time I heard my ex say the phrase "breaking and entering" to the judge in reference to me and the trespassing case. *Breaking and entering?* This was also where I learned that she had recorded our conversation from that fateful night. After this minor victory, where I witnessed how much some women can detest other women they know nothing about, I felt like this was all going to work out fine.

How could I foresee the depths of insanity to come?

The court date for the thornier dilemma of criminal trespassing was set, and I was in psychological purgatory: I still did not know the date, the location, or the "victim" of the alleged offense. I had a guess that this occurred in our building, from which I had by then removed my few belongings.

Ever helpful, my GF had actually sold a few items of mine on eBay in the short time I was absent. Yep.

We went to court in May, mere weeks after my March arrest. My lawyer told me that our judge may not be a favorable person for my case. She knew him and did not like him, but also told me that it was unlikely he'd be switched or replaced by another judge. I liked having that tough Irish lady for the previous hearing on the restraining order, as she'd made it clear she thought my ex was bad news, and cuckoo to boot.

Court day arrived, and I was relieved that this would be settled—once and for all. My lawyer did absolutely nothing; no work to find out anything at all about the specifics of my case, or as I had asked, whether this building had suffered another occurrence since I had left. Ominously, she intoned, "I think a case like yours is the hardest to work on. I actually think you might be innocent, and I'm always worried when my clients who are innocent get charged."

This sentence hung in the air like bad gas at a dinner party.

I was in the courtroom with a slew of small time criminals, mostly shoplifters. They'd steal from a department store, the store would send no one to prosecute them, and they would stroll out of court as indifferently as they strolled in. None were dressed up. I, on the other hand, was in a suit and tie, the only perp dressed this formally.

This was when I first met the two people who would have an effect on my immediate future. At last, I was face to face with the pockmarked arrogance of Judge Anthony Calabrese. He barely looked at me the entire time.

For the first time, I saw my accuser. She was youngish, early thirties, petite, and, I have to admit, attractive. I had never in my life seen her until this moment.

She entered the courtroom alongside my ex-girlfriend.

It turned out that neither of the arresting officers was present in court, necessitating another court date. The judge looked at my accuser. He was unfailingly solicitous to her, cooing, "Miss B, what do you do for a living? Oh, a teacher? That's an honorable profession; we need good teachers like you. Tell me, Miss B, when would be a convenient time for you to come back?"

He said nothing to me. Nothing. Didn't ask what my "profession" was, or what time might be convenient for me to reappear, and in fact seemed utterly dismissive of me.

My lawyer told me this judge had three daughters, one the exact age as "Miss B."

I was trapped, yes I was—not quite in hell, but far, far away from anything resembling a heaven.

How was I coping? Thanks for asking.

I was serving an apprenticeship while working part time, while getting my graduate degree, while starting my own brick and mortar business, something I'd never done. This activity and busyness were a good thing; I didn't have time to dwell on this matter all that much.

Then again, I was hopeful it would all end up well.

This nonsense about the arresting cops not appearing in court happened five more times. Five. More. Times.

What should have lasted a month stretched out a full year.

Seeing petty criminals slumping into court, while also seeing our finest, whom we pay to serve us, whom we pay to "show up," repeatedly derelicting their sworn duty, can make a man a tad bit cynical.

I felt like a damn fool in my shirt and tie, hands folded on my creased trousers. My lawyer was no help. She would often show up late, texting me, "Tell the judge I'm on my way!"

Bullshit.

On the court date before last, it appeared that perhaps due to repeated absences by the cops, my case was going to be dismissed. My lawyer in fact stood at the bench, turned around to me in court, and mouthed the word, "Dismissed."

The judge, having been in this situation before, let me know what he thought of me and my presumed "innocence." He said, "I realize this case has been dragging on for a long time. But," he said, looking squarely at me, "in no way am I going to dismiss this case, no matter what."

Through time-honored channels, he let the cops know they had to appear for the next court date, or else.

Every time I showed up in court, so did my ex-girlfriend.

Although she had nothing to do with this case, right?

It all came down to a do-or-die. In the week before the final trial date, I received some fresh, albeit bizarre, news. There was an element introduced into the court discovery heretofore unannounced: the alleged perp, me, had gotten into the woman's apartment by means of a lockpick!

I have a few treasured female pals I'm close to. When I updated them on this last development, this was what they said:

"*A lockpick?* Are you fucking kidding me? You can't even operate a key!" Another thing to note, gentle reader: my accuser was, in one version, exiting the shower, of course naked. In another, she was scantily clad but was about to enter the shower.

In any version, the end was the same: after picking a lock and seeing a young attractive naked woman, the man who was so motivated to break into a locked apartment simply turned around and walked away.

From another female friend: "I work on a lot of court cases as an expert for trials. One thing I know: if someone uses force or is motivated to 'break in' to a home, they are not going to quietly turn around and leave. That never happens."

But think of the timing. A creepy man happened to pick a locked door just as the object of his carnal desire was nakedly stepping into or out of the shower. Oh, the luck! The amazing timing! Cha-ching!

But then he thought, *"Meh,"* and walked away?

Does any of this sound to you like a bad Cinemax movie from 1992?

Another layer of clusterfuckedness—this man got out his lockpicking kit and proceeded to pick the lock on an apartment door just as the woman inside was strolling around naked—at 2:00 p.m. on a busy Saturday afternoon.

Wouldn't you suppose that someone, anyone, at this high-traffic time might have ambled by with garbage or groceries to witness a lockpicking-in-progress? No cameras? Hmm. So it's 100 percent circumstantial? As in, her word against mine? Huh.

Perhaps this is where I should mention that, at the time of this tragicomedy, I was comfortably into my fifties, with no criminal record of any kind.

If you were a creepy person who had picked locks to enter young ladies' apartments, would you really choose the middle of a busy weekend afternoon, the most visible time, with the highest traffic of all seven days and nights?

And upon breaking in, wouldn't you feel uber lucky to see her naked?

What are the odds?

Again, the luck, the stoopid serendipity! This was so damn stinky I actually was relieved. My lawyer would make mincemeat out of this woman.

Going into the final trial date, I wasn't assuming anything. Facts, such as age and lack of record combined with the sheer preposterousness of the case were encouraging.

Yet the judge afforded me zero illusions. Still, I had a lawyer, for God's sake, and I paid her money to help protect and speak for me in a court of law.

What were the "facts"?

- A man in his mid-fifties with no criminal record was never read his rights by arresting officers.
- The man was presented with no information on what, when, or where this misdemeanor occurred or with whom.
- No cameras were present. No witnesses.
- The alleged crime happened at 2:00 p.m. on a Saturday, in a hallway of a busy apartment building. The door to the alleged victim's apartment was locked but—in the middle of the afternoon—the alleged suspect got down on his knees and picked a lock.
- Only to find a woman walking naked inside at that very moment. Having picked the lock in broad daylight, and spying a naked woman inside, this perp simply turned and fled.

These are the facts the judge was presented with.

My ex-girlfriend of two and a half months, who tried and failed to place a restraining order on me, was side by side with the "victim" for all six court appearances.

Is this relevant, you ask?

THE TRIAL

Go time. Trial date. I was in my apartment once again tying my tie, polishing my shoes, and ironing my shirt. How did I feel at this moment? Should be happy that this was coming to an end, because I'd been through a long year of stress and confusion, but this judge was simply an asshole. An asshole with the casual power to wave his hand and change lives.

Going to court for any reason is never a picnic. Going on trial, being the defendant in a criminal case again and again with the metal detectors, the oppressive fluorescence, the slimy lawyers with too much hair product, the jokey cynicism of the court workers, the judge who reeks of self-importance—all of it beats you down. Some part of you vows to never travel near this fucking mosh pit again.

We all stand as the judge graces us. My lawyer, my accuser, my ex-GF, and their court-appointed public attorney, a young Asian man seemingly in his first year of community college, all face Anthony Calabrese, my judge and jury.

Finally, we're all together; even the arresting officers are present. Good to get the band back together. I'm virtually side by side with Ms. B, the woman who haunts me still. I'll spare the minor details and go for the bullet points.

Ms. B says this: "I was in my apartment, and I saw his face, the defendant's face. I saw it clearly. His face is etched on my soul." That's verbatim, btw.

She says this pretty convincingly, I must say.

My turn, but already I'm flop-sweating and quicksanding.

I manage to say this, in a voice not my own: "Your Honor, the first time I ever saw this woman, Ms. B, was in this courtroom, one year ago . . ."

My lawyer pipes up, earning her $4k by helpfully adding this: "Last May first!"

The judge could give a hang. It's amazing that I hired an attorney who didn't give a goddamn about my actual plight, my actual life, my future.

She seemed almost as hamstrung as I was in the presence of Anthony Calabrese. The court appointed prosecuting attorney—paid $4,000 less than mine—laid out the case: "Mr. Cogan taught a noon yoga class on Saturday afternoon, at Trump Tower [true] which ended approximately around 1:30 p.m. We know that Ms. B said the suspect was wearing 'comfortable athletic clothes,' which fit with Mr. Cogan as he came from teaching a yoga class. If he left Trump Tower at 1:30 p.m., that would enable him to travel home and place him at the apartment of my client at 2:00 p.m."

- If I ran, at a good clip, from Trump Tower in Chicago to our apartment, I would barely make it by 2 p.m. And to do this, to run or Uber it through city streets teeming with vehicles and pedestrians—after teaching a fucking yoga class, of all things— to my building, and then whip out my "lockpicking kit" while on my knees in front of a locked door at two o'clock on a busy Saturday afternoon—as in, broad daylight—is at the outskirts of doable, let alone believable.

Where in the name of God was my attorney? She uttered almost nothing in my defense in the face of what was by any measure preposterous, save for half-heartedly suggesting that perhaps my ex-GF and Miss B were in cahoots. And that I was kind of an old white guy with a spotless record. The judge was unmoved.

Here is an example of how ill-repped I was. The ex-girlfriend (you were waiting for her to make an appearance, admit it) steps up to the bench, clears her throat, and takes her moment in the sun.

She lives for this.

She tells the judge, "After I heard from Miss B about my boyfriend breaking into her apartment, I went to his car, and I looked around. I saw in the door well of the driver's side a tool kit of some type. I drew a sketch of the tool kit I saw in his car. When I went back upstairs, I googled what I had drawn in his car, and it came up as a lockpicking kit."

This is what's known in legal jargon as "perjury."

OK, dear reader, I implore you—tell me you, too, think this cannot be a real thing that actually happened. Can you possibly imagine that this absurd lie was left unchallenged? My attorney could have said something along these lines:

"Ms. X, how are you today? Good. Tell the court, in your own words, exactly how long it took you to apply your makeup this morning—

Objection!

Sustained; you may proceed, counsel.

So you went down to your boyfriend's car and you took a pad of paper to draw on, yes?

So you took the time to sketch out what you saw in the car's door well? I see.

Tell me, Ms. X, do you have a cell phone, a smartphone?

Ah, I see, you do. Tell me, do you ever take pictures on your cell phone? Ah, yes, as you are a young woman in modern America, you say you are obligated to shoot any number of trivial and vainglorious photos of whatever during the course of the day?

I see. So you possess a phone with a camera, one that works, is that correct? And you not only know how to operate that camera, but you in fact are quite adept at shooting photos with it? I see.

Yet, when it came to this most important matter, that of your boyfriend breaking into the locked apartment door of your neighbor, you didn't see fit to use your smartphone's camera to photograph the tools used for this criminal purpose? Instead of snapping several pictures, you took the time to draw a sketch on paper on your lap on the seat of the car? But you do not— am I correct—have these drawings with you today? Finally, are humans actually able to "google" a hand-drawn sketch?"

How many times have I rehearsed this counterpunch to the gut that never was? My lawyer was nightmarishly mute in the face of sheer insanity and ludicrousness.

I'll make this confession right here and now. I've succeeded in sublimating this story. To a point. Reading back what I've just written, I cannot fully believe this happened. But it did happen, and it's etched upon my soul. Much like my face was etched upon Ms. B's.

We take a break for lunch. I'm not quite there, not fully present and accounted for. This is how bad I was: after watching my ex-girlfriend and the accuser walk arm in arm out of the court-room, I sleepwalk to my car and drive to a local eatery. I park my car in front of a sign in the lot that says, "Any vehicle not checked into this lot will be immediately booted."

I read this sign slowly, possibly mouthing the words. I do not "check in." I get booted.

I eat a dead man's lunch and pay on a credit card to remove the boot on my car so I can go back to being on trial in front of a judge who disdains me, alongside an attorney who's birthed and wedded to the city stench, who's overbooked, overloaded, and under-principled.

I was present enough for this observation—when I got the boot, I sensed I was looking at a historic day in my suddenly long life.

Back in court. The air is bad. I have that feeling you get when you're on the losing end. Wishing I had someone in court with me, on my side. But I also just want to get through this.

We're in the final moments, and my lawyer has been AWOL. Just missing. Standing alongside, not with, me.

The judge asks for a book, one of those really old heavy ones, from the bailiff, to study the "precedents" for sentencing in a case such as this. He thumbs through the large musty book a few times back and forth. He ponders my fate, right in front of me.

Judge Anthony Calabrese addresses the court.

"Mr. Cogan, I find you guilty of this offense of criminal trespassing on Miss B. I don't buy that your ex-girlfriend is 'in on this' in some way, nor do I think your age or lack of any prior incidents such as this has any bearing in this instance."

He pauses for effect. He's doing his thing.

"But," he continues, "I'm troubled . . ."

My heart's pounding. I feel myself heading to that sunken place.

"I'm troubled by the leniency of prior sentences in cases such as this. I think for what you did, uh, Mr. Cogan, the precedents were too lenient for this type of crime.

I do find you guilty. I'm going to ask that you be placed on two-year supervision, but I'm bothered by the idea that each night Miss B has to look over her shoulder before she gets into bed, while you get off scot-free.

No, Mr. Cogan, I'm going to ask that you be evaluated as a sex offender. I'm truly bothered by this case . . ."

There is a film device employed in movies by Spielberg and Scorsese, where the camera moves away from the subject as the lens of the camera zooms in. It's used to show disorientation, and abject confusion. This was how I felt.

It's over.

The two ladies in waiting are almost dancing. They surely will dance when they're out of this godforsaken courtroom. My lawyer actually says this to me: "When she said your face was 'etched on her soul,' that's when we lost."

I cannot speak. I cannot. I can barely move or breathe, truth be told. It feels as though a hot dry wind is blowing through me, as if I were made of tissue paper. I have a hard time finding my footing, so acute is my disorientation. I'm in shock. Staggered to my marrow. The judge asks me if I have any final utterance, as if it mattered even a little. I hear myself shriek, *"I'm innocent!"* in a voice that comes from that sunken place, from that Kafka place. My lawyer gives me a look of pure pity. The rest clear their throats.

If the mark of a great defense attorney is the repeated ability to get guilty offenders off, then how do we rate an attorney who utterly failed to get a judge to declare that a middle-aged man with no criminal history, with no witness or evidence beyond circumstantial, posed—at a minimum—*a reasonable doubt of guilt?*

I shuffle out of the courtroom as if I were in shackles. I have few regrets in my life, recent or distant. But I goddamn sure as fuck regret shaking the hand of my lawyer just before we saw the last of each other.

THE FALLOUT

Immediately after the verdict and the mind-boggling request/ demand of evaluation as a sex offender, I went to the offices in the courthouse and was told what was required of me. I had to meet with a supervision officer once a month for two years and hand them a certified check of fifty dollars for the privilege.

This was where I first encountered a recurring scenario: after receiving shaming looks and disparaging comments from these civil servants, I would say, flustered and frustrated, "I'm in my fifties! I have no history of anything remotely like this! Do you actually think I'm guilty?"

Their answer was uniform: "Maybe you've been good at hiding."

My white privilege did me no good. I was merely a slick guilty creep—one who finally got caught, no less.

Paranoia metastasized through my mind like COVID. As someone raised Catholic, guilt was never hard to access. I had no such doubts about my minor conviction, as I knew I had zero to do with this woman and her phantom case against me. But being evaluated as a sex offender? That infested my psyche. Why? Did I suspect some deep dark shameful abnormality? Nah. I'm pretty much 99 percent hetero age appropriate. OK, 98 percent.

It wasn't some secret sexuality. I was snakebit after the past thirteen months of my life. I was in bizarro world, where I trusted nothing, no matter how logical. If all these insane events happened to me, how could I be sure this next thing would turn out fairly?

I put off being evaluated for as long as I could. I was always on edge, always paranoid. If a man was in a parked car outside of my business, I was convinced he was checking on me. I lived in a small coach house across from a playground. I could not go anywhere near there, and it preyed on my mind. Was I this thing, this pervert? What if? What if? Anxiety was getting the better of me.

The worst part of the paranoia was thinking, "What happens if I somehow get into some type of trouble?" I would now have two strikes against me. Suddenly I would have an actual record, a history.

A history.

I was cracking up. I went into a big-box hardware store. As I was checking out, the cashier suddenly got on the intercom: "*Code fifty-one* at register seven; code fifty-one at register seven."

I nearly soiled myself. "What's 'code fifty-one'?" I asked, completely zonked on fear.

"'Code fifty-one' means an associate will come over and tie your purchase to your car."

"Ah . . . yes, OK . . . got it. Very good. Carry on . . ."

This was where work, purposeful employment, proved invaluable. And, of course, the value of having people who care about you, worry about you, support and love you. Having the support and love of people who have known you for many years through all manner of successes and down times makes a life and death difference. On the night of my conviction and sentencing—officially the worst day of my life—my brother was on the phone, and he said simply, "You got framed."

It never occurred to me to frame this as I was in fact framed for a crime, one I had no knowledge of or part in. The oddest thing of all? To this day, I still do not know if the alleged trespassing of this woman I'd never met, who was strangely bonded to my troubled and dangerous ex-girlfriend, ever happened at all.

SEX OFFENDER EVAL

After weeks in limbo, the inevitable sex offender eval happened. My closest friends knew I was freaking out. They were not bothered (as far as I knew), but they hadn't experienced bizzarro world as I had.

I had a Friday afternoon eval with a doctor/evaluator who goes by the moniker "Dr. B." I had twice spoken briefly to him on the phone to set up the appointment. I could tell he was evaluating while we were chatting. I took immediate solace of sorts just chatting with him. He put me at ease and seemed to be a cool dude, like a guy I'd want to be friends with. I was encouraged but still wary.

Friday's eval day comes, and I'm pretty damn nervous. At least I'd had the fortitude to group text a bit of black humor: "Sure hope there's no math on this test." Just my way of saying "kiss my behind" to the world. I meet with Dr. B, and he's just as he appeared on the phone: cool and chill and easy to be with.

So begins an epic five-hour endurance test: five different tests, all with five choices (strongly agree, agree somewhat, no decision either way, somewhat disagree, strongly disagree). Five tests. One test alone had 525 questions. I'm not making this up. Eighty percent of the questions involved some form of this:

"I get excited when I'm in the presence of young boys."

The total number of questions such as this over five tests: 818. I counted. Added. Did the math.

Finally, it's just me and B in his office. I like him a lot. I'm actually relaxed while we speak for ninety minutes. Like with a shrink, except this one could end up putting your name on a public watch list. So a little different. We discuss my life, my attitudes, and my habits. I'm completely myself and not trying to "front" even a little. Just me. Example, when he casually asked if I was turned on by the idea of being with two women:

"Uh, hell yeah." I didn't demure.

At the end of a five-hour, 818-question ordeal, Dr. B says this to me: *"You're no sex offender. You're a normal guy, a good guy. A guy who got fucked."*

I'm stunned once more but this time in a healing way. I'm OK. I'm going to be OK. I ask him hopefully if I can be considered "no risk."

"There's no such category as 'no risk'; there's only high risk, medium risk, and low risk. You're extremely low risk."

I don't know what to say. I wasn't used to things going my way or even going logically.

Then he adds this:

"I want to tell you something. I see thousands of cases like this. This is what I do. In ninety-nine percent of the cases I see where someone is a sex offender, they don't look or act or think like you. Many times they have been abused in foster care or whatever, many have a low IQ and have mental/emotional issues, which are fairly obvious. But you? You got totally screwed by this judge. I'm really bothered and pissed off about your case because I'm a science guy—I look for facts, such as factual evidence in a case. This case was strictly your word against hers. No cameras or witnesses. How you, a guy your age, with no criminal history whatsoever, could be found guilty beyond any reasonable doubt is just plain wrong. You got fucked," he says once more, but I don't mind the man repeating himself.

This kind man was the first person to restore my sanity. To question who you may be "deep down" is the very definition of going down the rabbit hole. I was walking in a nightmare of paranoia and self-doubt on a massive scale.

Dr. B left me with these words: "Now, I think you should go up north to your home, have some Mexican food, drink a little red wine. You got screwed, but you're gonna be fine."

I've been living with this story for a few years now and didn't realize how much I'd put behind me, how much I'd focused on moving forward with my life as I knew it. If I can go through this experience and others mentioned previously and not hate on women as psycho money-hungry bloodsuckers (statistically the exception, not the norm), accept my own responsibility and blind spots, and cut myself some slack and move up and on, well, so can you. If I can encourage even one person who meets people online to do their damn due diligence, then I might ask, was it worth all that I experienced?

Aw, hell no.

In a world overflowing with irony, can you see the irony of *Rampant Douchebagery*? *I was indeed a dude sans clue*, but I wasn't the victim here. Why? I was busy getting on with my life, building a business, and getting a degree, despite my age.

Fuck it. Forgive your damn self. That might be step one—in life in general. Forgive and don't forget, but seek help in every conceivable way that moves you forward in this terrifyingly random and beautiful world.

Fall forward in life.

Which lens are you choosing to see through? Make new friends, ditch close-minded angry guys: it's all fear.

Ain't nothing to be afraid of.

To anyone who's been hurt, frustrated, disappointed, or worse, I challenge you to acknowledge—then activate. Stand up and shut down your D-Vices.

There are so many ways to engage in life.

Read an actual book, preferably from your local library. Volunteer for something besides more guy/beer stuff, as in "fireman for a day."

Make friends with a few women; they're often just as frightened and confused as you, but they talk about it and ask for help, as in acknowledge, then activate.

Buy a kayak, a yoga mat, some great running or hiking shoes. Take classes; start with cooking. Learn. Stretch yourself. Rescue a dog or two. Take walks in nature with them. Get a degree or certification for something you develop a passion for and bust your ass getting it, instead of feeling lazy and angry much of the time. Start dressing up and slimming down. Get a damn passport and visit a country you've been curious about on the spur of the moment.

Get outside your world and renew your soul.

CHAPTER 22
WAKE UP &
GET WOKED

126 AMERICANS COMMIT SUICIDE
EACH DAY. 101 ARE AMERICAN MEN.

Single white heterosexual American men are possibly the loneliest people on this choking planet.

Men in America are looking over their shoulder when it's the face in the mirror that calls. Trying to be a better man, a better father, a better neighbor and citizen is likely to be derided by the men who most need this book but will toss it instead.

We're talking about adult men who now engage in something entirely contemporary yet decidedly unmanly: trolling others.

Twenty years ago, no one knew what the word trolling even meant.

Enduring these fateful twenty-odd years, the divided states of America have been subsisting on a diet of cynical and utterly fake "reality" shows. Cynical talent shows wherein judges weep over mediocrity. Where Marvel comics have become our entertainment fertilizer, manure spread evenly over the land. Where cynical and formulaic music abounds. We've normalized the hamster wheel of cynical social media influencers, ultimately busted as frauds. All abetted by a cynical select few that are gambling on separating us from our common sense and decency.

Look, I don't know. *Screw that—I do know*. I know that we're in deep doo-doo as a nation. And I know that white heterosexual American men are mired in confusion. With that confusion comes rage, too often the go-to emotion.

See January 6, 2021. No, I mean really see it.

We're in desperate need of a course correction.

The first sentence of this book reads, "When did American men stop trying?" American men of a certain bent—let's say, perhaps an alt-right bent—are bringing our entire nation down down down.

Too many confuse kindness with weakness.

Too many are obsessed with not being a pussy.

Employing the term *woke*—currently connoted as evolving on issues—as a weapon against open-minded reasoning is emblematic of the nasty era we find ourselves in.

If you look around the social/cultural landscape, you might notice that there is a dearth, a dispiriting deficit, of not only decency but romance.

Romance is over in America, because only one side is participating. With each passing decade our culture gets more vulgar as it becomes less nuanced. More nasty and less tender.

How can pornography and romance coexist? One of 'em had to lose.

Which would you, a woman of America, rather receive from your partner: a written letter or a text/email of the same message? When was the last time a gent called you at night, and you spoke in the confessional dark for hours on end?

And while it's mostly the men who have driven this sad state of affairs, women are not without a role in this tragicomedy.

Generally speaking, the women and men who grew up trapped inside a world wide web seem to have lost something essential in their mix.

Younger women of today lack grace (roughly 100 percent of American women under fifty—as much as a dating profile represents—currently view the ability to be "fluent in sarcasm" as a favorable personality trait). Their male counterparts lack honor in their comportment.

"Comportment" is what this book is about.

Stand tall. Leave the cave. Toss your internet in the lake and look around. It's still a wonderful world, yet know this, men: you are needed.

Needed to be not just great, but good.

As suggested in the first chapter of this book, isn't it time for American men to be better? Isn't it time to leave the cave that imprisons you? Time to break free of those chains of fear?

Nearly two decades of research have rendered this burnished observation: far too many white American men are fearful and repressed grown-up boys.

What does it mean to be a "real man?" To be masculine and modern at the same time, what does that look like?

Face it, white heterosexual American men are threatened by just about every damn thing today. Women with college degrees who make $100k+ salaries and have their own homes and passports; "minorities" who have college degrees and make $100k+ salaries and have their own homes and passports. American men are stuck. Flummoxed. Paralyzed and atrophied.

I wish I could be more . . . cheery. There are people who would prefer to see a lovely bow and happy ending to this book you're reading.

But there's such a thing as toxic positivity too.

Women, raise the bar on acceptable behavior from your dates, BFs, and partners. Support them and cherish them but make them come correct.

Fellas, as if your life depended on it, seek love.

Find a great partner for life and cherish them.

Rescue an animal and cherish them.

Get off the internet porn train.

Ditch all internet sites that engender rage.

Learn how to cook, fly, dance, travel, volunteer—why remain lashed to the local bar with all the angry dudes? Unplug the computer—are you happier since plugging it in?—and immerse yourself in nature and give back to others around you.

Learn new skills, walk your dog, and look at the reflection in the mirror of your life.

Who, exactly, do you see?

ACKNOWLEDGMENTS

I've got a few folks who've helped push the rock down the road. First and foremost, to Dr. Catherine Marienau, for always believing, no matter what. It's doubtful this would have been written without your kind constancy. Special heart thanks to Julie Anixter, for saving (and "seeing") me at the eleventh hour. It's double-doubtful this book would have "come out" without your brilliance, belief and hard work. Melissa Wilson, you are a true angel, I'm lucky and grateful to know you. To my dear femme friends, such as Jessica Robb, Charlene Pratt, Kathryn T. Larson, Lisa Arsenault, Megan Devine: thanks, guys. To my beloved friends Mark and Eva Stevens, you were the first. Special thanks to the TOPOVS team: Marisa DeSalvio, Olivia Hack, and James Gallagher for diligence in all things editing. Thanks to Damian Jackson. Grateful shout out to the sweet artistry of Erik Holman and Black Box Visual.

Front cover photo: Donald Ford
Back cover photo: Thomas Mohr
Book designed by JC and Eileen Wagner

ABOUT THE AUTHOR

Instagram: @jamescoganwellness
Facebook: JamesCoganWellness.com
JamesCoganWellness.com
James@jamescoganwellness.com

Printed in Great Britain
by Amazon

51957055R00096